LOCAL MINISTRY

Story, Process and Meaning

Edited by
ROBIN GREENWOOD
and
CAROLINE PASCOE

First published in Great Britain in 2006

Society for Promoting Christian Knowledge
36 Causton Street
London SW1P 4ST

British Library Cataloguing-in-Publication Data
A catalogue record for this book is available from the British Library

ISBN-13: 978–0–281–05713–9
ISBN-10: 0–281–05713–3

1 3 5 7 9 10 8 6 4 2

Typeset by Graphicraft Ltd, Hong Kong
Printed in Great Britain by Ashford Colour Press

Contents

Contributors

The author of *Transforming Church* and *The Ministry Team Handbook*, **Robin Greenwood** writes from more than 35 years' experience of ordained ministry in the Anglican Church. After two decades facilitating learning and development for the Church's mission and ministry in Gloucester, Chelmsford and Wales, he is now Vicar of St Mary the Virgin, Monkseaton, Newcastle. He was a director of the Edward King Institute for Ministry Development.

Caroline Pascoe was brought up in one of the earliest ecumenical parishes in Oxford Diocese, England. There she was inspired by a vision of Christians using their gifts and working collaboratively with people of many faiths and none within the life of their local community and society. She taught in secondary schools for ten years, developing an interest in change leadership, which informed her subsequent work as Local Ministry Officer in Gloucester Diocese in the 1990s. In 2002 she became Ministry Development Officer for the Diocese of Llandaff and the Church in Wales. She has been a director of the Edward King Institute for Ministry Development and editor of the journal *Ministry*.

Ken Booth is Director of Theology House in Christchurch, New Zealand. After doctoral studies in Scotland, he taught at St John's College in Auckland, New Zealand. Later he spent 12 years as vicar of a parish in Dunedin. He has a keen interest in the theology and practice of ministry.

Robert Daborn is an ordained minister in the Church of England. Over the past 20 years he has been serving in the Diocese of Lichfield as a parish priest, Local Ministry Advisor and, latterly, Director of Local Ministry. He is strongly committed to developing the ministerial gifts of the whole people of God. He has recently moved to a new post on the staff of the West of England Ministerial Training Course.

Jenny Dawson is an Anglican priest currently serving as Vicar of Pauatahanui in the Diocese of Wellington, New Zealand. As a lay person, she was a member of the commission that produced *A New*

Zealand Prayer Book. For many years she has worked in ministry education, both in policy development and as a practitioner, at provincial and diocesan level. From 1991 she was priest-in-charge of a parish that chose to move into Total Ministry, so from that time she became deeply involved in the development of local shared ministry models.

Adrian Dorber became Dean of Lichfield in September 2005; prior to that, from 1997, he was Director of Ministries and Training in the Diocese of Durham. He has been involved in the UK Local Ministry Movement and currently chairs the Planning Group for the UK Local Ministry Annual Consultation.

Daniel W. Hardy was Van Mildert Professor of Divinity at the University of Durham and Residentiary Canon of Durham Cathedral, and subsequently Director of the Center of Theological Inquiry in Princeton. He now teaches and supervises, especially in ecclesiology, in the Faculty of Divinity at the University of Cambridge.

Christopher Honoré is a priest in the Auckland Diocese of the Anglican Church in Aotearoa, New Zealand, and Polynesia. He is a history graduate with a strong interest in nineteenth-century mission in New Zealand, especially that involving the North German Missionary Society. He has worked in ministry development and ministry education and formation in the Waimate Archdeaconry since the mid 1990s. Christopher is committed to assisting faith communities move from understanding themselves as communities gathered around a minister to being ministering communities.

James A. Kelsey is Bishop of the Episcopal Diocese of Northern Michigan. He previously served as a ministry developer in the Dioceses of Vermont and Oklahoma and for ten years as the Ministry Development Coordinator in Northern Michigan before his election as Bishop in 1999. He has been a consultant with numerous dioceses throughout the USA, Canada, and New Zealand, and has co-ordinated an international network of ministry developers over a number of years. He currently serves on the Standing Commission on Ministry Development for the national Episcopal Church, providing leadership in major revisions of the Ministry canons, and is co-convener of the Standing Commission's Committee on Theological Education.

Phil Kirk is a principal lecturer in Organization Studies at Bristol Business School in the University of the West of England, Bristol. His own background has been in industry, and later in the public services, working in the health service and then in higher education. He has a long-term interest in Africa, where he has been involved in educational and leadership projects with the British Council, and in partnership work with African churches. His interest in education is in working with people who are prepared to look at their own ideas and actions and explore the potential of learning (the possibilities and limitations) for creating personal well-being and beneficial social change.

David Leslie is Assistant Director of Lifelong Learning in the Diocese of Liverpool and Vicar of St Cuthbert's, Croxteth Park. After having constructed a training programme for the Liverpool Ordained Local Ministry Scheme, he completed his doctoral studies with a theoretical presentation of the components of experiential learning and an evaluation of how the students were changed by the course. David believes that being able to think critically is fundamental for the development of a local collaborative ministry that seriously wants to engage with contemporary society.

Tim Morris has served in congregations in the Scottish Episcopal Church since his ordination in 1975 and is now Rector of the Church of the Good Shepherd in Murrayfield, Edinburgh. For nine years he worked as Dean of the Diocese of Edinburgh alongside Bishop Richard Holloway. He sits on the Provincial Mission and Ministry Board and Home Mission Committee, where he holds the Local Collaborative Ministry portfolio.

Martin Oxley trained for ordained ministry at Edinburgh Theological College, and served his curacy in St Mary's Cathedral, Glasgow. He then worked as priest-in-charge of a UPA parish, also in Glasgow, combining that job with being Director of Studies in the Theological Institute of the Scottish Episcopal Church (TISEC). He has been Rector of St Magnus, Lerwick and Priest-in-Charge of St Colman's, Burravoe, in the Shetland Isles since 2000. In all these roles, Martin has been committed to encouraging the ministry of all the baptized and empowering people to reach their full potential.

Tom Ray has been baptized for 69 years and was the eighth bishop of the Episcopal Diocese of Northern Michigan. His academic studies brought him out of the backwoods of Michigan to the University of Michigan and the General Theological Seminary in New York City. For the National Church he served on the Standing Liturgical Commission for nine years and participated in the 1988 and 1998 Lambeth Conferences. He is now retired.

Peter Sedgwick is Principal of St Michael's College, Llandaff, a priest in the Church in Wales, and teaches in Cardiff University. He was previously Vice-Principal of Westcott House and sat on the Church of England's Board of Social Responsibility.

Anne Tomlinson, a permanent deacon serving within the Scottish Episcopal Church, worked for nine years as Tutor in Practical Theology in the Theological Institute of the Scottish Episcopal Church. For the past three years she has held the post of Provincial Local Collaborative Ministry Officer, encouraging the ministry of the baptized in Episcopal congregations across Scotland. Her passion for 'doing theology with the whole people of God' sprang from working in a Base Ecclesial Community in Bolivia in 1984.

Preface

The essence of this book is the search for clues for how to be Church now as an echo of God's own activity and ways in the world. Across the centuries the Scriptures continually evoke Christian community living as a true performance of the good news which Jesus preached and brought near, and which the first congregations were inspired by the Spirit to embody. At a time when the Church is often small and vulnerable there is a natural temptation for it to seek security in the past or to lay on itself more burdens, expectations and practical devices for perpetuating inherited patterns of existence.

This book is a combination of celebrating, reporting and investigating the meaning of the energy and hope released in recent decades by collaborative ministry and mission and the formation of intentional Christian community. 'Local', 'total', 'mutual', 'shared', 'total life caring' and 'collaborative' mission and ministry are ways of labelling approaches to Church envisioned as the people of God working together and sharing responsibility for the mission that God has entrusted to them.[1] Taking as its source the intrinsically communal nature of Christian faith and the gift of the Holy Spirit forming each local church and disciple in Christ, Local, Total, Mutual or Collaborative Ministry has made an important contribution to the Church's capacity to serve the movement of God's life in the world.

This book also celebrates and completes the important work of the Edward King Institute for Ministry Development (EKI). EKI, a network of practitioners, trainers and practical theologians, pioneered new approaches to church development, which have now largely been drawn into the bloodstream of the Church. EKI became a network of clergy and laity committed to reflective practice, developing continuing ministerial education (CME), ministerial review, vocational discernment for disciples, linking the disciplines of leadership and organizational theory with pastoral and strategic thinking and practice. Its journal *Ministry* adopted an interactive model, inviting guest editors to draw data on new practice together with interdisciplinary reflection. Its editorial board made a deliberate choice to avoid formal academic writing, choosing instead to encourage holistic reflection in dialogue with the contributions of other journals.

In the last decade EKI has made a series of contributions to encouraging the healthy and creative development of Local Ministry: National Consultations at High Leigh (1994) and in Leicester (1998); a Lambeth Conference meeting on Local Ministry for the Church's mission (1998); and publications by members and directors, including Robin Greenwood's *Practising Community* (1996) and *The Ministry Team Handbook* (2000). Caroline Pascoe and Robin Greenwood, the then directors of EKI, were also involved in leading and speaking at the International Symposium on Local Ministry in San Francisco (1999), attended by bishops, ministry developers and Local Ministry team members from across the world, including a number of EKI members and friends. As a final piece of work by the Institute, the Board invited the directors to edit this collection of reflections on practice, partly as a response to the findings of the 1998 National Consultation on Local Ministry.

Crucially, this report concluded that Local Ministry is a key element in the Church's strategy for ministry and mission now and in the future. Flowing from this conclusion, the report raises key issues identified by consultation participants for urgent and collaborative work by dioceses and the Church as a whole. These include:

- the need to continue articulating a vision for being Church;
- the importance of theological work at every point of scale on participation in the mission of God within the whole of creation and to counter tendencies to focus merely on the internal life of the church congregation;
- a commitment to learning from other disciplines, such as sociology and social anthropology, spirituality and management, and from each other;
- the development of appropriate educational and learning processes related to context, valuing local experience and offering tools to enable people to reflect on and learn from their experience;
- the need for attention to diocesan strategic planning and practice. The report reflected that 'Dioceses will need to ask questions of their own practice such as "Are we really owning and articulating a strategy worked through in every part of our life and decision-making?" "How are local churches being resourced for their

mission in their particular contexts?" "In what ways is the diocese providing monitoring and appraisal and how is it being received?" "In what ways does the diocese listen to the experience of local churches?" "How far do diocesan relationships and processes model collaboration?" '

- effective systems which enable responsible decision-making to be shared are needed. 'They will require sensitive listening, and skill in enabling local people to articulate their insights. They will need to move beyond systems of formal representation which are often cumbersome and time-consuming.'

- 'As ministry is increasingly shared by laity and clergy, the nature of ordained ministry and the task of the clergy needs to be re-stated to relate to the new situation.'

- the spreading of models of good practice in the selection, training and appraisal of teams.[2]

At the time of writing, it is clear that much of this work remains to be attempted. However, at the 2005 UK Local Ministry conference, held at Durham, a number of working groups were established to take forward many of these issues.

This collection of short reflections gives snapshots of imaginative developments in some parts of the Anglican Communion as well as formulating questions about the future identity of the local church. These reports of work attempted in varying contexts are offered as a stimulus to further developments elsewhere. Our hope is to encourage scripturally, contextually and theologically resourced investment in mutual patterns of mission, ministry and community development for the strengthening and deepening of the Church's part in the coming of God's reign in the world.

The final piece is by a leading contemporary Anglican theologian, Daniel Hardy, who, ever generous in his support for younger writers, has contributed immensely to the process of thinking how to be Church now. He brings a perspective that respects the urgency and committed endeavour of the practitioners and offers leads for further theological critique and stretching.

Robin Greenwood and Caroline Pascoe

Notes

1 Edward King Institute, UK Local Ministry Consultation Report, 1998.
2 Edward King Institute, Consultation Report.

1

On the way: Choosing commitment

ROBIN GREENWOOD

The practice of community

The contemporary world's story is one of violence and exclusion at a time when the Christian Church in the West and in North America is experiencing humiliating challenges. A variety of forms of Church certainly are prospering: the sharply focused, eclectic, often suburban, 'mega church', some exceptional parish churches redeveloped and led in untraditional ways, and cell churches of many kinds, that recognize a desperate need for intimacy and belonging. However, in the face of most people's bored disengagement with organized religion, we experience both the complacency of preserving outworn routines in the local church and institutional panic that the old order is slipping away. The statistical research, notably of Bob Jackson, reveals that the digging deeper of old lines of thought, even in confident and well-organized churches, is failing to stem a growing malaise. The judicious use of such approaches builds insights gently without fostering resistance towards those whose detached observation could merely add to the shame of failure among practitioners locally.

As a movement, 'Local Ministry' has offered a theological and practical response to the contemporary situation by evoking the urgent need for deliberately interrelational and inclusive practices of gospel community. The intentional performance of a corporate Christian faith has the potential to show people, societies and nations what, against all the odds, is possible through trust in God's persistent love revealed in Jesus and energized by Spirit. In recent decades, ecumenically, the notion of a mission-orientated Church has emerged in which many realize that every worshipper has a part to play in the widest meaning of being Church. Dioceses have voted for missionary visions based on the rhetoric of collaboration, rooted in New Testament images of being called to live and work in relations of mutual love. Christian communities are learning to understand themselves consciously as continually formed by the set of stories that constitute the Jewish–Christian tradition. What is called for is a new response to God's unpredictable faithfulness through being formed over and over by the stories of Israel and Jesus. Nourished as a contrast model of community, the agenda of God for a peaceable kingdom in a world of fear is a much-needed alternative practice of being human. The need is for urgent debate that avoids the human tendency to be adversarial or scornful.

A Church that lives through dying and rising

The practice of such community, however, more than a polite democratization, has at its heart the new life that comes only through Christ dying on the cross, raised by God releasing the Spirit, connecting every person with God's life. Dying in order to rise is often overlooked for what it is, a non-negotiable and constant theological foundation for doing Church. A world that experiences and is aware of so many forms of intense darkness and tragedy needs a Church that has the courage (within its own life) to face and hold pain and ambiguity as well as warmth, hope and appreciation. One of the invitations to the churches offered by the Local Ministry movement is to allow themselves to be gently broken from proud pasts and to be open in ways that can meet the world's lament, as well to learn from their own shortcomings. As we struggle positively to know how to be animators and leaders within, rather than dominating or substituting for, Christian community, clergy and lay leaders are invited to move from the habits of control and fear of innovation.

The need for an imaginative idea

The imaginative idea of Local or Shared Ministry serves the Church prophetically when it subverts the temptation to become merely a project, the whim of a bishop or blueprint committee response to a problem. The Church in successive ages reinvents itself within fields of factors and possibilities, in which transcendental values, experience, pragmatic pressures, continuity with the past, theological reflections and hope play a part in varying measures.

When in 1996 I first published *Practising Community: The Task of the Local Church*, I referred to international and ecumenical principles of theology and practice, notably regarding the trinitarian character of God revealed by Jesus and many meanings of *koinonia* (such as community and communication) worked out in various contexts. Among the authors who galvanized the shaping of this vision stood Leonardo and Clodovis Boff, Bonhoeffer, Dussel, Ecclestone, Gunton, Hauerwas, the Lima texts, Metz, Moltmann, and Schwöbel and Zizioulas. This momentum stimulated the inexorable building up of new ways of imagining how to be Church. The primary example I offered, from my own experience, was that of the Diocese of Gloucester. At that time it had had the benefit of ten years of episcopally thought-through and led, consistent and dedicated development of Local Ministry. Initially and often controversially, this was triggered by a theological response to the Lima texts on *Baptism, Eucharist and Ministry*, studied in parishes across the diocese, in market towns, inner city, urban villages and rural parishes. Later, as in many dioceses in the last decade of the twentieth century, a team of officers were commissioned by bishop and synod to foster and critique Local Ministry development, respecting the widely differing contexts.

Since then, many bishops and dioceses in the UK, and throughout the world, have adopted various forms of Local Ministry. However, what has often been avoided is a rigorous theological and spiritual struggle to know what is being proposed and how this links with our understanding of God, God's mission in the world and the purpose, character and authority of the Church. The dangers of losing the imaginative idea to mere institutional routines and structures have been vastly underestimated. The process of weaving the practice of Local Ministry as a liminal interpretation of church praxis, rather than merely a pragmatic quick fix or even the new establishment, has been precarious. The Anglican love affair with clericalism, and the defining of limits of competency, creates the tendency for Local Ministry to be seized upon and repackaged to shore up inherited but exhausted patterns of Church, rather than primarily to be an enzyme for constantly re-finding how to be a community that reveals and serves God's mission. When irritated bishops vent their frustration on development officers who don't 'deliver' sufficient 'teams' the case is made. Similarly the theologies of God, mission and Church of which Local Ministry is a practical expression are undermined when newly appointed bishops merely dismiss work and processes that have taken place years before their own arrival or when bishops preaching at inductions comfort parishioners by merely reinforcing expectations of former patterns of lone clerical ministry.

A never-ending journey

The continual process of finding how to be Church actually is Church. An inherent and perpetual characteristic of Church is the dissatisfaction that reformulates its own practice – constantly reinterpreting the originating event, as indeed Jesus and Paul were themselves instrumental in reforming the Jewish tradition. As human beings we need enormous personal maturity to avoid clinging to a particular idea or orthodoxy that once served us well. The God of travelling expectantly, so vibrant throughout Scripture, invites us to leave the dead to attend to their own funeral arrangements. Recurring reform movements, integral to the self-critical identity of the tradition itself, so easily become an end in themselves or some new part of the furniture. Their purpose, rather, is continuously to assist the Church in its task of reassessing its own performance as a response to the current situation and to God's dynamic activity in the world.

One way of telling the Church's story is as endless, overlapping and often contradictory renewal movements. Each one engages passionately with Scripture, liturgy, discipleship, baptism, social reform, evangelism, relating faith to work, education and deepening intimacy with God in worship, prayer and study. The Parish and People Movement, Worker Priests and the Edward King Institute are examples of time-limited, intense activity and writing emerging in particular moments, inviting the whole Church to reinterpret some facet of its understanding and practice. Once a new way of imagining or experiencing has dawned, and accompanying activity integrated, the movement has done its work and the Church moves on, enriched and eager for reform in other areas. The influence for reinvigorating the field becomes absorbed, but is not to be equated with the field itself.

The Local Ministry movement, perhaps because it touched on so many aspects of church life (mission, ministry, liturgy, spirituality, discipleship in the everyday) was from the first tempted to solidify as the new face of Church rolled out in expensive schemes, rather than making its contribution and letting the flow of energy move on.

That energy is already partly integrated and refocused in parishes and deaneries called, in partnership with dioceses, to engage in Mission Action Planning, through renewed ministerial partnerships between laity and clergy, always depending on particular circumstances, resources and responsibilities.

Context specific

A common critique of Local Ministry is that it has a 'one size fits all' mentality. In *Transforming Church: Liberating Structures for Ministry* (2002), I deliberately described and discussed five quite different, though theologically related, working models of collaborative ministry in the UK, North America, Australia and South Africa. I demonstrated the value of a trans-disciplinary approach, including the study of Scripture, liturgy, theology, organizational theory, psychology and social anthropology. Essays in this present collection point to determined and flexible experiments in this field. At their best they are fusions of the needs and resources of a particular context, dialoguing with the most appropriate developments in leadership and organizational theory, and rooted in an unquenchable desire to serve God's coming reign, a critical loyalty to so many past experiences of Church, and a risky openness to the astonishing and gracious presence of God now.

Echoing the Trinity: radical difference in dynamic unity

The gift to the Church of Local Ministry, in diverse forms, is the challenge to become more explicitly responsive to the *perichoretic* relationality that constitutes the Trinity at work in the whole of life. We need to avoid the danger of colluding with a tendency to use vague trinitarian speech to refer to a generally friendly church. Crucially we note that all speech about God is mere analogy so that extreme caution is required. Second, we are referring to speech about God that describes a relatedness of difference in communion. There is no prior unity or differentiation, only a co-intentional and simultaneous differentiated oneness. The identity of each person of the Trinity is formed precisely within the activity of relating. It's about a practice of Christian community engaging with the vitality of the wild and destabilizing presence of God, uniquely offering hope for the flourishing of the world and its people. Subversively it challenges habits of thought, especially around restricted performances of power, success and human life together.[1] The outpouring of energy that is Local Ministry means the Church can never be the same again. It exposes complacent, nostalgic, painless ways of Church that offer simplistic, comforting, politely laughing niceness and nostalgia. It emphasizes the role of Church to promote spiritual communion between the baptized and the Trinity, to make community through preaching, confessing, celebrating in the Eucharist, and being led by apostolic ministers. In uniquely different canonical structures, local churches are also called together to be the visible communion that God is and desires. At the heart of such community lie relationships of forbearance, tolerance, a care of mutual interest, love, sharing in the body of Christ, being at one with the poorest, and sharing gifts both spiritual and material (Acts 2.44).

Serving God's mission

A Church that serves God's mission will be shaped by two interconnected purposes.

The first is the deliberate choice to become an embodied example of living the good news of Jesus as a direct response to the Lord's Prayer, 'your kingdom come on earth as in heaven'. To be Church is joyfully to point to the end time (*eschaton*) when humanity and the whole creation will be fulfilled in Christ through the Spirit for the Father.

The second is to think out in very practical ways how to be ordered or shaped by a conscious discernment of and engagement with the content of Christian faith that serves God's own mission. In its internal and external relations, a local church practises that quality of relationship that is a sign and foretaste of what God will have when God's passionate desire for all creation is fully satisfied. Such a church is the first shoots, the early blossom of God's *shalom*.

The question has to be faced: do mainstream churches really have the will to be truly open to all? Their inherent character easily degenerates into being elitist, narrow and unable to serve those in need except through patterns of patronizing subordination rather than through mutuality and transformation. In recent years a steady stream of publications has emerged on evangelism and on reviving, planting and growing churches. However, the immense silence in this literature on the contribution of Local Ministry raises important theological and spiritual questions for this study. Can evangelization truly be effective unless the Church repents of dealing in the colonial language and practice of exclusion rather than embrace? Is there a readiness to abandon patterns of paternalism or the heritage of dependency on clergy? Do we have the nerve to let go of confident, linear, and controlled programmes? Is the vulnerable and relational concept of God's life and power at the heart of Local Ministry in fact unpalatable? Do we prefer the safer paths of individual consumerism to the risk of taking the more authentic paths of walking the way of the cross?

Central to the longing of God and a population weary of unconvincing public religion is the need for ways of performing the faith that intimately connect. This means a renewed learning that balances body, mind and spirit, a closeness with God that draws many into widely differing journeys of prayer, resulting in Christian groups that become more vulnerable to people and a world God passionately desires. Sharing the Peace in the liturgy has very little to do with the natural friendliness of the worshippers. Rather, it is an active prophetic symbol of the miracle of growing in Christ and a renewed commitment to God's coming kingdom. Against all the odds, this group of very different people have come together once again to praise God and through grace and the inspiration of the Word to choose to stand against all that brings Christ to the cross. Here a resurrection people pledge to work for God's peace in every weekday opportunity, near and far. This sign of inaugurated eschatology tells the world the new beginning is here; together we shall work for God's good end (Eph. 1.10; Col. 1.20; 1 Cor. 15.28). Routinely we mutter before receiving the body and blood of Christ, 'only say the word and I shall be healed'. But do we want to be healed? Do we expect to be transfigured, today or any day? The Church's work is complementary to but categorically different from that of other caring organizations, yet we are afraid to witness explicitly to God and to expect the freedom of our growing into what God loves us into becoming.

Churches find joy and peace when the pattern of their ordering is becoming consistent with what has been shown to us of God's emancipating, loving movement, exchanged between the persons of God's self and with the entire cosmos. The mystery of God is largely incomprehensible to us, though all have access to some part of it, through worship, personal experience and suffering. To speak analogously of God as 'Trinity' is to utter the impossibility of speaking of the creator God simply as one alone. The diverse and competing images for God that erupt within the faith tradition (such as companion, king, liberator, physician, gardener, mother giving birth, hovering bird, or rock) hint at the elusive God often known in absence or elusively, through footprints. This rainbow of names for God, none of which alone satisfies, is increasingly mirrored in current imaginative and participatory liturgy as a journey towards becoming like God (e.g. Taizé, Iona, silence, contemplation, drama, and services of the Word). This stands in contrast with patterns of 30 years ago, when all the baptized were expected to find their place within a homogeneous eucharistic celebration.

The portrayal of God the Holy Trinity, as unique persons in relation, is growing in its influence on the future of the world, the shape and task of the Church and the practice of ministry. 'Relationality', a stronger word for the purpose here than 'relationship', is a characteristic of God's own life and a paradigm for God's kaleidoscopic intention for the fulfilment of the cosmos. This theological perspective challenges those pervasive forms of human and Christian living founded of life based on adversarial opposites, the permanent subordination of one by another, and the legitimating of patterns of hierarchical domination, however benign.

A trinitarian ecclesiology has the capacity to evoke patterns of mutual love or friendship. 'Friendship' in this context is not about the complacency associated with similar identity but with the creative tension that becomes available when opposites offer mutual respect at their borders and in hospitable process allow themselves to become more than the sum of their parts. Friendship, as a portrait of radical partnership or mutual co-intending, holds the possibility not only for bypassing old dualisms but for offering hope for the flourishing of neighbours, societies, nations and the justice and peace of the world. To love and be loved in divine *koinonia* friendship is to build a house in which all, whatever their human status, are received in mutual, reciprocal love that prefigures the final, ecstatic condition of all in God.

The title *On the way: Choosing commitment* summarizes the argument of this essay that rests on discerning a connection between the practice of Church and the communion of diversified connectedness that is the trinitarian life. Freedom and commitment are two sides of the same coin, rather than irreconcilable opposites. The meaning to be found through deepening communion (*koinonia*) with the dynamic *perichoretic* life of God requires that we negotiate and maintain the tension between the seeming opposites of freedom and commitment, chaos and discipline. Rather than proposing a dialectic between coercion and liberty, we choose the unique quality of order (chaordic) that is a mirror of God's complex, reciprocal, trinitarian life. A simple example is the vocation of the sculptor. The inevitable decision to choose a medium, e.g. to work not in paint or charcoal but in granite, is to accept a limitation but to expect a glorious result. Or take family life. The work of parents and grandparents is certainly to love all the children in the world, but very specifically and creatively to hold in unique, patient and mutual regard the particular children of this family in which we now live and in which, through suffering and patience, we also find our flourishing.

So what kind of church practice emerges positively from the choice to accept God's chaordering as a particular set of values, particular people and places as the location for growing up into God's life, embracing our fullest possibilities in the search for the world's final flourishing? I shall conclude by briefly hinting at possibilities for exploring this freedom and commitment through the images of Church as a community of love, authenticity, abundance, learning and character.

1 Community of love

One of the perennial questions in a community of love or friendship is: how is authority to be exercised? After centuries of benign, if often cavalier, hierarchical control, there is as much danger in denying that churches need leadership. A vital approach to this question lies through asking whether the Church is practising Christian faith in the exercise of authority or uncritically importing inadequate models from elsewhere. The work of thinking, reflecting and praying about this is especially urgent in this time of the 'democratization' of the Church.

Theologians and mystics agree that our striving for success and control can be precariously based in pride, fragility and grandiosity. The real journey begins when we allow that the only proper starting point is that of knowing that the God who creates us in freedom and love is the one who initiates. Before we turn to God, beyond our imagining, we are already regarded and beloved. The practice of Christian community provides a home where we are invited to know how deeply we are loved, as temples of the Holy Spirit. We begin by giving up on having to make life work well through our own determined effort. Like the returning prodigal our only way is to receive the embrace and luxurious welcome of the Father. Then we are released to risk losing life to find it in following Christ. At the heart of the gospel there lies only God's pattern of loving, which is infinite, sacrificial and life-giving, respecting our freedom 'to death, even death on the cross' (Phil. 2.8).

How much the world needs churches that are deliberate and tough communities of the new order of love. The hope that Christians bring to society lies precisely in the fruits of being formed through a deepening love affair with God. So we are free to become formed in, and called to show and tell the truth about, living. In all the mess of the world, churches live and invite others into the way of life, called and infused by Christian faith, in which they are shaped in their own identity and anticipate how God will one day reconstitute all things.

In public corporate performance, churches show the world the truth about persons and about relating through making visible the truth they find in the speech and action of the God of Israel and of Jesus. In theatre, ballet, dance, poetry reading and musical expression, there is no higher calling than to performance that is freighted with the values and love of writer, performer and participant. Understanding with body, mind and spirit is demonstrated in rehearsed, strenuous, risky and demanding public practice. The saying, writing, preparation and presentation are all equally parts of the performance or drama. Similarly, within the discipline we call Church there will be suffering as well as joy, intensity as well as relaxed enjoyment, thinking and worshipping, telling out and demonstrating.

2 Community of authenticity

Sharing in the mission of God, churches reach out to the contemporary world, caught up in individual fears, wants, needs, preferences, and fantasies. Christian community practice offers access to a deeper existence born through 'losing one's life'. In Christian theology and practice, dying to self is the way to find true life (Matt. 16.25). Mistaken identity lies at the heart of so many of the world's tragedies.

Christian performance offers instead the way of *kenosis*, deliberately letting only Christ be seen in us (Phil. 2.9–16).

The world needs Christian communities of those who are learning what it means to be free: that is, those who are on the way to becoming real or authentic.

Knowing that we are the beloved of God makes it possible to set out on a tough journey which takes us to a level of awareness some have called the 'True' or 'Essential' Self or the 'Real' I. Being able to monitor our lives is to access the human gift of 'self-reflective consciousness', deeper than everyday awareness. The twentieth-century spiritual pioneer Thomas Merton describes the potential in everyone to know the 'diamond' blazing as a point of pure truth, 'the gate of heaven' in each person.[2] Empowering Christian community living is an invitation to break through, step by step, into a greater sense of our authentic or real authority as Christians and as leaders. A spiritual guide writes, 'To end the bizarre tyranny of the ego is why we go on the spiritual journey, but the resourcefulness of ego is almost infinite and it can at every stage sabotage and pervert our desire to be free of it.'[3]

3 Community of abundance

Dying to self is the only way to resurrection, and this process strikes a mortal blow at the dominant myths of society. The world of mendacity presses us to want more because we do not have enough. Christians practise a community life of abundance, as those who have left everything behind in order to follow Jesus. The servants of Jesus Christ experience God's near-overwhelming blessings; in their reframing of life they are filled with abundance, pressed down and running over. Letting go of defences and gradually relinquishing every false security, privilege and attachment is to put on Christ who shows us God as a defenceless baby and as a man in his prime, stripped, beaten and crucified.

Three theological pointers remind us of the abundant and relational energy to which God invites our response.

Koinonia

A deep principle of Christian community living is that Christ is the unfailing source of our love, energy, prayer and capacity to serve.

Although the world holds selfishly to possessions in case they run out, God brings us to our present situation through an initiative that is not ours, though it means a sharing in immense 'beatitude', joy, transfiguring gifts, and participation in Christ's suffering. A theology rooted in the highly suspect notion of 'communion' (*koinonia*) had become a vital key to understanding the nature of the Church. Communion was recognized as a central Old Testament theme. It reveals the unfolding of God's invitation to humanity, created in God's likeness, into relationship, followed by the breakdown and renewal of this relationship (Gen. 12.1–3; Exod. 19.5–6; Deut. 12.5; Jer. 31.31ff.; Isa. 49.6 and Mic. 4.1–4). The New Testament portrays God restoring the broken relationship through Jesus and the company of those who are in his mission. In the power of the Spirit, the baptizing communities witness to the restoration of communion with Father, Son and Spirit, through the ministry, death and resurrection of Jesus.

Sharing in Holy Communion makes community. The Eucharist becomes the focus for participating in this renewed relationship in the body of the Spirit-filled Christ. Communion with the Father, through the Son, in the Holy Spirit actually makes the Church. The Easter mystery creates a communion in which all human barriers become meaningless and relationship between humanity and creation is restored (Col. 1.15–20; Gal. 3.27–9). Through the continuing working of the reconciliation made possible in Christ, in the sacramental life of the Church, the human fraction of communion can be healed (Matt. 18.15–20). The New Testament recognizes the tension between the brokenness of disciples and the hope of the perfecting of creation. The celebration of Eucharist is a first taste of that peace which will come at the end of all things. Sharing the Peace liturgically can be a powerfully effective symbol of the local Christian community pledging itself once again to allowing itself to be used by God as a vehicle for bringing in the kingdom values of the gospel – through the everyday acts and relationships of the Church in its neighbourhood and in the world.

Diakonia

The contemporary hymn, 'Sister, brother, let me serve you, Let me be as Christ to you', is a reminder that Christian community practice deliberately models mutuality in a world where people are sold into slavery, treated as objects for gratification and seduced into debt by the greed of others. An International Consultation on *Diakonia* held in Larnaca, Cyprus, in 1987 defined *diakonia* as the 'active expression of Christian witness in response to the needs and challenges of the community in which Christians and the churches live'. Christian love includes the global dimensions of facing oppression, environmental destruction and the struggle for justice and peace. The Christian task of *diakonia* is to be for the world a performance of mutuality, so that no one regards themselves as separate from the poor and we do not pray for 'those who are in need' as apart from ourselves. This work includes working to further empower those who are especially at risk and who have little voice in society and staying with them the extra mile. The diakonal character of the Church must lead to active sharing of resources that enhance the quality of living, always respecting the desires and insights of those we serve and seeking to transform and oppose all that stands in the way of justice.

Friendship

God's trinitarian essence offers the original and rich image of friendship. Genuine friendship cannot exist where one partner is identified as merely passive or needy. Human friendship with its potential for mutual, authentic love, as between David and Jonathan (1 Sam. 18.1, 3–4) or Lazarus, Martha and Mary (John 11), is a window into the communion that characterizes God's trinitarian life. As a metaphor for God, theologians Elizabeth Johnson and Sallie McFague speak of intimate companionship and friend. Gentleness, compassion, openness, unconditional love, reverence and care for the weak are traits of the biblical God in whom we may confide as with a friend. Johnson, reacting against classical descriptions of God, retrieves the biblical notion of Sophia, Wisdom, as making everyone friends of God and prophets (Wisd. 7.27). By the Holy Spirit we become God's friends and discover delight, conversation, joy and security. In friendship with God we discover a reciprocity and mutual regard that breaks the old patterns of authority. Instead of practising patterns of diminishment, churches witness to the possibility of speaking and acting in terms of the flourishing of all through being befriended in order to turn to others and to the world as sisters and brothers in liberating friendship. The close affinity of humanity with the earth, an inescapable ecological theme throughout Scripture, has been recalled in Christian feminist writing on friendship. Notably, Elisabeth Moltmann-Wendel demonstrates how inseparable is the friendship between God and God's people and the diverse human experience of 'the secret power of God's earth'.[4]

4 Community of learning

St John invites us to be made free by the truth (John 8.32). The task of the local church that practises *koinonia*, *diakonia* and friendship to make a new world is to enact the meaning it finds in God. To be effective in its purpose, the Church must school all its participants in the basic rhythms of faith that we may all learn to keep God's time. If Church is a corporate performance, we shall need disciplined time to learn how in our uniqueness we may best participate. As with all performers of art, engineering, poetry or astronomy, being Church requires disciplined practice, knowledge of first principles, obedience, and involves the suffering of a good performer, who has given their person to the total performance, become possessed, taken out of self, self-forgetful, in order to excel at performing the good news of God's redeeming love in Jesus Christ. As we have seen, an essential part of this learning is the absorbing, in body, mind and spirit, of the trinitarian grammar that speaks of and creates a life of mutual inclusion. This is the vocation of Christian community.

God seeks to transform the whole person, to enable us to become more compassionate and more genuinely humane. Learning for the coming reign of God involves the integrated self: that core of our being that works as a centre for understanding and valuing: where rationality and feeling, memory and perception are not opposed. There is a story to learn and to live in with fidelity. This requires rapt attention and willing receptivity, a growing alertness to the movement of God's grace in our deepest parts. To become skilled performers of the faith is to learn to dance Christ's dance. Dancing may not be a frequent activity for us. Imagine being gently and laughingly cajoled into standing up and taking part in the ceilidh of the kingdom. In the music, the good spirit and the learning from others, we find our will overcome in that no longer can we help ourselves. The musicians, the music and the dancers take us to themselves.

At last the Church is discovering that learning is not the privileged preserve of grey scholars and gifted teachers. It's a many-sided, mutual and transformative process and always a co-operative enterprise. It is created by community and it forms community. Instead of the clerical leaders alone, all are now called to be the faithful in the critical knowing and preserving of a heritage and to be active in the communication of its wisdom. Such is the essence of any form of Christian discipleship. And where such a desire for learning becomes a reality, fear – and its partner, ignorance – cannot flourish. Unfortunately many clergy and laity have been damaged and shamed by theological education to the point that they are wary of participating and doubtful of its value.

Now is the time for creating communities of wisdom, in which all the baptized can be liberated by study, and all can learn and teach. Learning needs to be linked with themes we have already explored. Involvement, mutuality and accountability are essential for learning to be a performing community of faith. This will involve compassion and love, not previously associated with mind-focused education.

Summary: Community of character

This collection of reflections challenges the tendency towards seeking merely pragmatic solutions to problems within Anglican (and other churches') attempts to be the Church today. To take a social trinitarian theological approach to being Church that serves justice, peace and the world's future in God's hands is to set aside many inadequate assumptions about how people relate within and on the border of churches with neighbourhoods and the wider world. Despite several decades of thinking, talking and practising 'Local Ministry', in the UK and in other provinces, there remains a determined resistance to re-examining fundamental questions. Churches in change need to dedicate posts and finance to sustaining expertise and prayerful thought. Mere training is inadequate unless combined with theologically resourced envisioning and education. Leaders of this movement have often been misunderstood, marginalized or treated as a threat to the powers that be. Our hope is that these contributions will serve as a reminder of the importance of treating with consistency and pastoral care those who care passionately enough to persist in asking vital questions about the development of Anglican ecclesiology and polity in the twenty-first century.

If a thoughtful and God-focused debate on matters of substance were really taking place about the future of the Church's ministry, whenever a new collaborative ministry or support team is being licensed by a bishop there would inevitably be placards and demonstrations in the churchyard, with protesters remonstrating 'Our church will never be the same again.' How subversive is this apparently soft and inter-weaving theology and practice that challenges inhabited patterns of imagining and speaking of God and the forms of authority that God legitimates. There are those who insist that, in order to maintain the spirit of Anglicanism or the Church we love and respect and must hand on to others, certain elements must be safeguarded. For ex-ample, unless we are to be accused of abandoning our inheritance we must have as many stipendiary clergy as possible scattered across the land; we must have certificated courses in individual discipleship that fail to foster local and corporate learning; at all costs we must license a plethora of individual diocesan ministries from the bishop rather than from within the local church or deanery; supine worship must be led according to the prescribed forms; small congregations, keeping expensive and unsuitably furnished buildings open, must be ministered to by overstretched clergy licensed to 'look after' just one more church; house for duty is promoted as a cheap way of keeping more churches ticking over; in a hierarchically ordered diocese, un-paid (non-stipendiary) clergy are treated as a lesser form of priestly or diaconal life, requiring less commitment and a less rigorous train-ing; and 'growth' in terms of more people attending church comes to be regarded as the only worthwhile measure of the value of any particular church or the success of any clerical ministry.

There are no answers or orthodoxies about how to be Church in postmodern society. There are only deep, transcendental principles by which we must work – relationality rooted in Trinity, *koinonia*, seeking justice, and demonstrating God's freedom and open love equally for all. Every church is called to be a learning community in which there are no off-limits places and so requiring skilled ministries of facilitation, listening and teaching. With one eye on God and the other on society we shall find new expressions of Church. Protect-ing priesthood, pews and privileged authority is the opposite of vul-nerably and joyfully performing the gospel of Jesus Christ. Changing society requires the telling of a new story, singing a new song. The Church's choreography, in public worship, parish life and organiza-tion, is of a New Heaven and a New Earth. In a desolate farming situ-ation where just staying longer is an achievement, someone paints the outside of their house garishly and extravagantly buys a honky-tonk piano.[5] Extravagance and celebration rather than duty, passionate love rather than grim accounting, speak more of the Church for which we have been finding both rhetoric and practice.

All practices and people are dynamically driven with contradictions and fail to achieve their potential. In an age of such despair, research, strategizing and lack of genuine communication among the churches, now is the time to put God and Christian faith at the centre. In every age the only task of the Church is to be one, holy, catholic and outreaching in, with and for the sake of all, to show the world its true life. The Local Ministry movement, like all others, playing its part, is high on aspiration and rich with stories. As we recount and attend to some of these in later chapters of this book, our need is to move on from looking for security in success or failure, praise or blame and to stay close to the dynamic of God's trinitarian life. The careful attention to knowing God in all things, the holy mystery pervading life in all its minute detail, deeper than we have so far dared to go, must be our starting point.

Local Ministry is nothing in itself but it is a way of asking the right questions. What kind of Church might we become if intimacy with God, present, open to all and active in all places, were to become our greatest desire? As Jesus showed, to be his friends is in fact riskily to be friends, even to death, with everyone, especially the excluded, on the way to the messianic feast. How can this be worked out in the Church's life at its many levels?

Notes

1 Robin Greenwood and Hugh Burgess, *Power*, London: SPCK, 2005.
2 Thomas Merton, *A Merton Reader*, ed. Thomas P. McDonnell, New York: Image Books, 1989, p. 347.
3 Sogyal Rinpoche, *The Tibetan Book of Living and Dying*, San Francisco: HarperSanFrancisco, 1992, p. 117.
4 Elisabeth Moltmann-Wendel, *Rediscovering Friendship*, London: SCM Press, 2000, p. 124.
5 Michael Frost and Alan Hirsch, *The Shaping of Things to Come: Innovation and Ministry for the 21st-Century Church*, New York: Hendrickson, 2004.

2

Congregational learning in Shetland, Scotland

MARTIN OXLEY AND ANNE TOMLINSON

1 Telling the story

Shetland today

To the northeast of Scotland, located at latitude 60° north and longitude 1° west, Shetland is a chain of more than 100 islands (15 of which are inhabited), stretching nearly 90 miles from Muckle Flugga in the north to Fair Isle in the south, with a coastline in excess of 900 miles, and covering an area of 567 square miles. The population of Shetland is 23,000, the largest proportion of whom (7,500) lives in the capital, Lerwick (298 miles from Edinburgh, 211 from Aberdeen, 598 from London and 225 from Bergen, Norway).

The North Sea oil industry has long been recognized as a key component of not only Shetland's economy, but the economy of the UK as a whole. In Shetland this is reflected in three main areas: the Sullom Voe oil terminal, offshore oil and gas fields and the services related to both of these. Despite the relative decline in the role of the oil industry within the Shetland economy, it still accounts for a substantial proportion of local economic value. The largest contribution comes from the combined output of fish catching, fish processing and salmon farming. Agriculture and knitwear represent other traditional industries, while tourism accounts for a significant proportion of the economy's value.

In addition to its social and economic profile, Shetland celebrates a diversity of culture, history, language and identity that make it distinct from Scotland and the rest of the UK mainland. These have been shaped (and continue to be formed) by geographical location, environment, climate and demographic change as much as they have by oil, isolation, accidents of history and Vikings. Shetland is also a lively human community, faced with many within the range of the social issues of mainland Scotland.

St Magnus Scottish Episcopal Church, Lerwick

Shetland has always been rich mission territory, and the ecclesiastical landscape of Shetland today reflects something of that insurgent history. In Lerwick alone there are congregations from a dozen different Christian denominations. The Scottish Episcopal Church was re-established in Shetland in 1861 (after an absence of more than a century) thanks to the notable efforts of a priest, Robert Walker, and the sympathetic support of some local landowners.

St Magnus was created as a mission church in the mid-Victorian era, at a significant point in the social and economic development of Shetland. In particular, the enormous boom in herring fishing transformed and dominated life in Lerwick from 1870 until the outbreak of the First World War. The herring industry had an impact on local life of a similar order to that of North Sea oil a century later. Patterns of social life, work and employment, wealth distribution, travel and communication were constantly in flux. The response of the Scottish Episcopal Church was to establish a school and mission outposts in the areas of seasonal and occupational population growth, working especially among seafarers and fisher-girls.

Consistent with its history, in recent years St Magnus has rediscovered something of both its missionary roots and its missionary purpose in seeking to discern its purpose at the beginning of the twenty-first century.

Development of a mission-based perspective

What is really significant about this next section is the liminal and contingent detail of the process. It acts as a clear reminder that Local Ministry can never be conceived as a product or laid out like an airport runway. Its process has to be faithful to the interactive life of God, waiting in patience, respecting the local, listening to the diocese and wider Church, reading the moment, and exercising love in freedom, reciprocity and lack of domination. Writing in *The Scottish Episcopalian*[1] about the development of Local Collaborative Ministry in Shetland, Joan Sandison, a member of the St Magnus congregation, said that '*it is hard to remember at what point the process of change really began'.* And so it is. Vitally, there was no blueprint, no ready-made programme or formula that was available to be applied to the situation of the Lerwick congregation of St Magnus. There was no one specific meeting at which we all sat down and said that we would now 'do' something called 'Local Collaborative Ministry'.

As we look back at how we have got to where we are, it is import-ant to remember that what has happened has emerged from the process, and to disentangle its origins would be no simple task. The positive outcome is that, as should be true of any church, the congregation is simply learning to be itself, responding to its call, and seeking to know how to live its life. As some have observed, this pattern of ministry is not novel but merely what used to be known as 'dis-cipleship'. Reflecting now on what we have come to see as the Local Collaborative Ministry (LCM) programme at St Magnus, one mem-ber of the congregation has said:

> [The LCM programme] has made us think about our own local sit-uation and the direction we would like to move – involving all aspects of the church – fabric, spirituality, finances, development – everything that is needed. [It] challenged us to think about how we interrelate to achieve these. We're now able to discuss openly and disagree with-out hurting one another.

Stewardship

If we were to put a date on the beginning of the current process, we would probably look back to a congregational conference in March 2000, held at Spiggie in the south Mainland of Shetland. The key issues at that congregational gathering were patterns of worship, the ordering and structuring of buildings, sustaining pastoral care and stewardship. This set an agenda for action over the coming years, though the subsequent resignation of the rector for a time pre-vented the formulation of any strategy for implementation. The Spiggie Conference and the appointment of a new incumbent were followed (in 2001) by a highly successful and participatory steward-ship campaign. This raised congregational giving to a level which meant that finance no longer dominated the agenda, freeing the church to turn its attention to mission. In the financial years between 1999–2000 and 2002–3 the annual income of the congregation rose by 86 per cent.

The stewardship campaign was important, [reflects one member of the St Magnus congregation] for it meant we were no longer worried about the church closing. Vestry [church council] meetings had been taken up with finding the next month's salary, so hadn't had time for faith things . . . Why did the stewardship campaign work so well? The people may have been important. We were delighted and elated after the stewardship campaign. I find myself saying that church is quite exciting at times!

'Making your church more inviting'

When we were invited to 'explore the gifts of the congregation' I couldn't imagine what she meant, but I now see! My gift is possessing persistence, which has a negative as well as a positive aspect. Weaknesses may also be gifts.

At the end of 2001 and the beginning of 2002, St Magnus undertook the Foundation Phase of the Provincial Mission 21 programme, 'Making your church more inviting' (MYCMI).[2] A team of members of the congregation worked through nine sessions of the course with a facilitator appointed by the diocese. MYCMI is an exploratory process allowing for the consideration of new possibilities for the church, and the laying down of the groundwork for subsequent discussions, decisions and plans within the life of a congregation. One of the results of the course is to identify several goals to be proposed to the Vestry that will then help to shape and form work in the future. In order of priority, the St Magnus MYCMI team identified the following goals.

1 First, the team celebrated the leadership given by the rector, and proposed continued support for the 'shared participation' already introduced by the rector (e.g. lay participation in worship). They also appreciated that because of the geographical factors affecting the ministry of the Episcopal Church in Shetland, there might be a critical point when the pastoral care currently given by the clergy would need to be shared by the laity, and that this point might be reached sooner rather than later. Appropriate lay training would be required for the various tasks.

2 The stewardship campaign had identified many of the 'fringe' members, and following this the team suggested that different ways of approaching and establishing the needs of these members be considered, with a view to meeting any needs that might be identified

with firm proposals for the implementation of appropriate action (including setting up worship in areas outside Lerwick).

3 Social events were recognized as playing an important part in the life of the church, especially in reaching out to 'fringe' members. It was proposed to issue a yearly calendar of events, to be followed by personal invitations to key events.

4 The team suggested the setting up of a 'gatekeeper' (or sides-people or stewards) rota with some training for 'gatekeepers' in the welcoming of new people, and in addition the identification of a small number of members to form a team of welcomers.

5 The team recognized that no provision was made for children, and that they would wish to propose the development of a children's corner in church, and the setting up of a Sunday School for any children joining the congregation.

6 Acknowledging the fact that there were no study groups, house groups or teaching sessions, the team aimed to set up a group for St Magnus members.

These six goals, identified by the Mission 21 team, were presented and discussed at a special meeting of the Vestry. The Vestry gave unanimous approval to all of the goals, and agreed that they would form the basis for action.

2 Analysing the story

Implementation

Agreeing to adopt six goals as the basis for your action in the future is one thing; actually doing something about them is another. The Vestry therefore agreed a process of implementation to try and ensure that the various aims and objectives did not get lost.

Each of the goals required a different sort of action over varying timescales. Some could be implemented almost immediately, and some would take several years to develop. For example, we could establish a children's corner in church (Goal 5), a team of 'welcomers' (Goal 4) and an events calendar (Goal 3) very soon, but deepening and developing a pattern of shared ministry (Goal 1), and continuing to identify a response to the needs of the congregation (Goal 2), were seen as part of a much longer-term process. Achieving Goal 6 depended on the emerging outcomes of Goals 1 and 2.

Goal 1: Shared ministry

> I've learned that what we're all doing is ministry . . . St Magnus has
> always suited me fine – but there was a hierarchy – so that we only
> helped when asked. This has changed quite a lot – people now come
> forward to help and therefore they feel more fulfilled.

Emerging from the Mission 21 process, therefore, was a clear commitment to the development of a broadening pattern of ministry. This
was both exciting and daunting. Some found the idea threatening.
In order to begin to work out what we actually meant by this, a small
working group was set up to bring some ideas back to the Vestry. Quite
quickly, discussion within the working group helped to identify that
'shared participation' was not simply about what we do at the Sung
Eucharist on Sundays, nor involvement in pastoral care only about
'helping' the clergy, but about the church's whole pattern of mission
and ministry. A member of the working group has said this:

> Ministry is about putting into practice what you speak about in
> church – whether in a small or large way. It stems from a genuine con-
> cern and love for people. It is done freely, for no reward. It is the right
> thing done for the right reason. If someone falls over in front of you,
> you don't think twice about helping them up. Ministry should be like
> this. If it becomes a chore, it's not real ministry. It's a natural response
> . . . Help given without goodwill is a negative experience – for both
> giver and receiver.

Therefore, rather than answering the more closed question 'What
tasks need to be done, and how do we train people to do them?' we
needed to ask more open-ended ones:

- What is the mission of the Church in this place?
- What ministry does that mission require?
- How do we enable as many people as possible to participate to the
  maximum of their potential?

In asking these questions, it was recognized that the answers may
as yet be unclear. However, for the life of St Magnus to continue to
grow and develop (as Goal 1 required) we needed to engage with these
questions. In itself, this conclusion suggested a further stage in the
process of the development of participation in the life of St Magnus
that the Spiggie Conference (spring 2000) and Mission 21 (autumn–
winter 2001–2) had begun to articulate. That is to say, we needed to

ask ourselves more clearly 'Why?' before we could answer 'What?', 'Who?' or 'How much?'

Following the first meeting of the working party (February 2002), and in order to investigate the means by which this further stage in the process might best be done, the rector took advantage of being on the Scottish mainland to meet with the Bishop of Aberdeen and Orkney, the Local Collaborative Ministry Officer for the Scottish Episcopal Church, the Mission and Ministry Officer (Diocese of Moray, Ross and Caithness) and the Mission 21 Co-ordinator (Diocese of Aberdeen and Orkney). The rector outlined the situation thus far, and asked for advice on the best way to proceed based on any other experience in the province.

In order to help address the questions, 'What is the mission of the Church in this place?' 'What ministry does that mission require?' 'How do we enable as many people as possible to participate to the maximum of their potential?' it was suggested that a process be run over the following nine months with three interweaving elements: the person in context, faith in context, and mission in context. The way in which we would involve ourselves in this process remained to be clarified, but at the end of the nine-month period we hoped to be in a position to identify the areas of training and skill development that we needed to help take our work forward. We proposed that such training and development work would best be done under the heading of a Local Collaborative Ministry (LCM) project, supported by the diocese and the province.

The Vestry agreed to such a preparatory programme to help us address these three questions. The outcome hoped for was that we would be able to be clearer about our training and development needs, and that this would allow us to implement some form of Shetland-specific LCM project. The Vestry believed that such a process could only strengthen and deepen the life of the congregation, and were excited at the potential for development.

'Person, faith and mission in context'

Thus was born the first year's programme of work, entitled 'Person, faith and mission in context', which ran from August 2002 until June 2003. The foundational tenets of the programme were that we should better understand ourselves and our context, as the basis for understanding our mission. Set within the pattern of the Church's

year and our own social and fundraising events, the programme aimed
to reinforce an understanding that our baptismal vocation is lived out
in all aspects of our lives, and is for everyone. It therefore included
a variety of ways of working together and learning. It was open to
all. It tried to model what it was attempting to be. The programme
also included an important point of principle: that of review and evaluation which in turn led to new action and a new programme. Such
a cycle is now built into our way of being and has helped us to measure our growth in qualitative and quantitative ways.

'People on the move'

At the review at the end of the first year's programme (June 2003),
we realized that our initial plan to complete a nine-month preparatory course and then look at training and skill development was hope-
lessly unrealistic. Our reflection helped us to see that the process we
were now embarked on needed to continue. Initial questions had led
to new ones; our journey of discovery had allowed us to begin to
see our priorities and ourselves differently. Our whole way of being
together had changed. And so out of that reflective stage in the cycle
came 'People on the move', the title we gave to the second year's programme. Initiated in 2003, 'People on the move' has had as its focus
the second of the three original questions, 'What ministry does that
mission require?' In turn this was reviewed and evaluated in June 2004.

The benefit of such review is that it allows the process of dialogue
and honesty to develop. 'Even the unhelpful sessions seemed helpful – sometimes it was painful!' 'My theology is a growing thing: it's
a learning curve but like a spiral – I keep coming back to some of
the same questions. What's going on is great – we question what we're
doing, and who we are.'

During a recent informally structured survey of the congregation,
one member observed that the impact thus far of the LCM experience
on the congregation as a whole had made it more faith orientated,
harder working, more collaborative, more caring of its members, more
questioning and more focused on St Magnus.

> These answers reflect the stage we're at. We're building up a basis
> from which to operate – a church can be too inward-looking and go
> nowhere. Now we've confidence in ourselves and our abilities, which
> we didn't have before, so that we can go out.

Each of the two years' programmes has been resourced by the Provincial LCM Officer and supported by the Provincial LCM Committee. The programmes have also been sponsored by the Diocesan Mission Committee, since our geographical disadvantage makes it very hard for visiting teachers, speakers and facilitators to be here. Over the last two or three years we have built up a body of people who regularly come to be with us, thus maintaining a consistency of contact, a continuity of development and a building of relationship. Shetland is not a place that you go to do 'a session' and then go home at the end of the evening. Shetland requires you to stay. This is an important element of living with the development, and has been of enormous benefit to St Magnus.

The support that has been given to this work has allowed us to proceed with confidence, not under threat of closure or reorganization, but of our own free will because we believe that this way of becoming the Church is the best way for us. We probably do not know what we will look like in years to come, but we are committed to the process, recognizing that we have already changed our way of being.

> LCM is not a package that can be given to any congregation to work in the same way as here. Each congregation has their own unique needs, structures, relationships, possibilities for growth. It's important not just to be a congregation that exists to exist – this is very inward-looking and selfish. The desire to make the faith more meaningful for growth is important . . . It's an ongoing process.
>
> The [LCM] process in the sense of journey was most important – whatever it was about. It's like being prepared for going on a journey – so we have to be prepared for the journey of self-discovery. We have to have the right material, leadership and setting. The process couldn't happen without this. Setting doesn't matter [in itself] – if it did it would put faith and process in question. The process was tailored to meet the needs of the context and the people at this point in the setting.

Growth and change

> Our confidence has been kept alive because of a feeling we have to prosper. The Sunday School and the coming of new young families has heartened us . . . People have emerged who are willing to give of their time and talents.

Unexpectedly in 2002–3, the congregation of St Magnus began to increase in size. Whereas an average attendance on Sunday might have been 30–35 people, it has grown to be more regularly in the order of 50–60. The total number of communicant members is 118 (the highest since its oil-related peak in 1982), and the number of adherents is 150. A combination of communicants, adherents and other associated families and individuals gives a total membership of 310. Particular areas of growth have included the number of pre-school children using the Children's Corner, and the choir with new and younger members. This has gone hand in hand with an influx of people coming to Shetland to work, returning to live or looking for a different church.

All of this is greatly to be welcomed, but requires us to change and develop as we grow – as any healthy organism must in order to survive. We are on a threshold that brings with it many opportunities and some dangers. Our current systems might break down and the growth become unsustainable. How we develop will require sensitivity and skill. Such response has already begun with the development of the crèche and changes within the life and work of the choir, but there are other issues about how we welcome and care for people, and a whole range of other questions that will mean change.

We have created a Mission Co-ordinating Group (MCG) to tackle some of the issues of size transition as creatively, efficiently and effectively as possible. The MCG comprises a representative from each of the Mission 21 goals (shared ministry; outreach; social events; welcoming; children) as well as other aspects of our life: music, 'housekeeping', communication and administration. The Vestry also has a representative, to maintain a specific link between the bodies. One of the members of the MCG acts as Chair. The rector is a member. The membership of this group is not to do all the work, but to encourage and co-ordinate the work and ministries of others.

The MCG will in effect act as an executive agent of the Vestry (having tasks delegated to it by the Vestry). The MCG will report to the Vestry. In turn, the Vestry becomes free to exercise an oversight of all aspects of St Magnus' life without having to become involved in minute detail. The Vestry will also have more time to tackle the core issues of building maintenance, restoration, fundraising, finance and so on. As we grow, these matters will require a greater amount of work.

3 Reflecting upon the story

Looking back at the story so far three characteristics emerge.

Mission-led

First, it has been mission-led. If one considers the issues which were being addressed at the Spiggie Conference of 2000, it is clear that the well-being of the congregation was uppermost in people's minds, namely how worship could be better ordered, buildings maintained and members cared for. All important and laudable aims, but all *internally* focused. The decision to run a stewardship campaign in the following year was a significant first step in the developmental process, for not only did its organization involve many from the congregation, thus increasing lay participation, but it raised giving to the point where the congregation attained a measure of financial security. With this in place, the Vestry was freed from the shackles of maintenance-led agendas and able to begin to look outwards in new ways, a movement that was further strengthened by the congregation's subsequent engagement in the MYCMI programme from the Mission 21 portfolio.

This nine-session course energized people into considering their apostolic calling, encouraging them to think about how they might become a more welcoming, open and inclusive community. The Local Collaborative Ministry programme has taken this process a step further, calling members to be active and conscious agents of trans-formation at God's invitation wherever they are situated, both as the gathered and the scattered people of God; the raison d'être of the programme is about increasing the participation of the baptized in God's programme of mission, and not primarily about adding to the congregational roll.

Corporate and participative

Second, it has been a process that has sought to involve the whole congregation in formation, not just a select few; it has been corpor-ate and participative. This pathway was intentional, the result of a deliberate choice on the part of the Vestry. Back in 2002 when the MYCMI group reported that the new missionary focus outlined above would require greater lay involvement in ministry, the natural inclination was to select two people who were heavily engaged in parish work and sponsor them to train as readers. Had this course of action been followed, the candidates' training would have distanced them from the congregation. It would have removed them physically for long periods of time, as much of the training would have occurred on the mainland. Perhaps more damagingly, though, such privileged access to formation and training would have set them apart from the rest of the laos in another way, too. Returning thus trained to the sponsoring charge, while no doubt being an invaluable 'help' to the rector and the self-supporting priest, their presence and actions would simply have shored up the old ecclesiological paradigm; the congregation would have seen them as lay providers of pastoral care, worship and service, and thus continued to remain as passive recipients of others' ministry. Little would have changed; the triangular shape of the church with a disempowered laity would have soldiered on.

These dangers were, however, foreseen and the much braver decision was made to enter into a process of congregational formation, offering theological education and skills training to all. In a book entitled *The Rise of Professionalism*, Magali Larson has commented that 'education is now the main legitimator of social inequality in industrial capitalism'.[3] Similarly, the way in which *theological* education, deliberately or otherwise, has been handled by the Church has made it, likewise, the main legitimator of *ecclesial* inequality, creating a sense of disempowerment among the non-ordained members of the laos and militating against a round-table ecclesiology. In general, theological education has been offered only to a few, those selected for ordination or those training for authorized (and highly clericalized) lay ministry, who thus become seen as 'the knowledge professionals'. William Countryman has powerfully reminded us of the mistakes churches can make by restricting theological education to the clergy.[4] This restricts reflection about faith and life merely to the clergy and reinforces divisions between clergy and laity. Consequently the laity, without active theological dialogue with the clergy and suspicious of theology, apparently beyond their grasp, resort to making decisions without the benefit of the rich Christian tradition that remains a clerical preserve.

Countryman goes on to chart the dangers of such restriction: an unreflective laos, cut off from the riches of the Christian tradition, unable to think theologically about daily life and prone to sliding down the slopes of fundamentalism.

It is one of the tenets of Local Collaborative Ministry, on the other hand, that participation in such theological education should be the birthright,[5] and obligation, of all baptized Christians. Indeed a recent report on 'Theological Education in the Anglican Communion' recommends that:

> all Christians are called to learn Christ and that theological education is one way of describing an obligation that discipleship imposes on every member of the body. Every Church should aim to provide opportunities for all its members to study the wisdom and truth of Christ in relation to their own culture, vocation, interest and capacity... theological education is fundamental to the renewal of Anglicanism today. It is the means by which wisdom – the learning of Christ by the power of the Holy Spirit – is developed in the Church, and directly serves the practices by which the Church sustains itself in its mission in the world. Theological education is committed to bring[ing] each person to full stature or wholeness in the mind of Christ by continuously developing in them the dynamic of Christian wisdom.[6]

Similarly a report closer to home, *Formation for Ministry within a Learning Church*, commonly known as the Hind Report, states:

> Theology [understood as knowledge of God] is inseparable from faithful and believing discipleship. Theology as such is thus vital for every Christian, and even though clergy might properly be expected to be theologians, this is not a professionalism that belongs to them alone ... Although candidates for ordination may reasonably be expected to possess a particular expertise in theology, the foundations of this expertise lie in the common faith of the people of God and should be developed as part of the whole Church's commitment to learning and being equipped for service.[7]

It develops the idea of the Church 'as a school of theology', listing the benefits that would accrue from such an 'increase [in] the level of understanding among the generality of Christians'.[8]

In accordance with these beliefs, the programme of formation and skills' training that was set up in St Magnus (2003) was thrown open to every member of that congregation. Those who have not yet attended any of the sessions are kept informed of the content of the material studied through sermons, comprehensive magazine articles and addresses at the AGM; the process is at the heart of the congregation's life, and is not an added extra for the keen.

All-encompassing

Third, it is a programme focused on the whole of a disciple's life, not just the churchy bits. All too often congregational life discounts, and even negates, the experience and expertise of its baptized members, making it seem as if the only knowledge and praxis that is worthwhile is that which is contained within the ecclesiastical world.[9] And well-meaning programmes purporting to be concerned with the liberation of the laity actually end up shackling them in quasi-clericalism. As Celia Hahn writes:

> Lay ministry is not recognized as different in direction from clergy ministry but takes as its model the liturgical and pastoral functions ordained ministers perform. The vested acolyte, standing by the altar; the lay pastoral associate, seeing ministry as kindly support of individuals – these helpers may be performing useful and rewarding services. But if these roles are seen as the typical and primary expression of lay ministry, the real distinction between clergy and lay roles loses its distinctive direction and fades into a support system for clergy ministry.[10]

The St Magnus programme emphasizes the enabling of members of the body to identify their God-given gifts which they employ daily at home, in the community and in their workplaces, as well as in the gathered congregation, increasing their confidence in the use of the same. One of the most encouraging responses to the programme so far is the account of how engagement in the sessions had helped a woman 'find voice' as a beloved daughter of God. That, in essence, is what liberative and transformative education is all about.

4 Learning from the story

It is too early to fully assess the programme of formation and training which has run under the auspices of both Mission 21 and Local Collaborative Ministry these past three years; the process is ongoing and will continue to evolve as it does so. Nevertheless, periodic evaluation sessions have been built into the programme, so far using the Church's Provincial Competency Framework as a monitoring tool,[11] and from these episodes the following five points of learning have emerged, which continue to influence the Local Collaborative Ministry's thinking and planning.

1   The first and most important point of learning is that it is good practice to take the process slowly. The shift from a priest-led model of Church to that of a learning and ministering community in which all are equal participants, committed to growing in understanding and living our their baptismal calling,[12] cannot be achieved in one easy step. Rather, the process is analogous to the laborious manoeuvres involved in turning a tanker in a narrow channel; in order to face in a new direction, the craft must proceed in a series of repetitive movements, and as many hands as possible are required on deck throughout the procedure. Experience from elsewhere in the Anglican Communion had alerted us to the fact that 'a parish will need at least seven years to make this shift',[13] and thus the St Magnus programme was predicated upon this wisdom. In terms of the format of the theological education being offered to achieve such a shift, it is clear that linear curricula, courses of study which progress from a set beginning to a set end, do not suit the educational needs of congregations with their ever-changing membership, varied needs and widely differing capabilities. Instead the programme has been designed on a spiral basis, in which familiar material is returned to in an ever-deepening way, and this is clearly meeting the need of participants.[14] The sessions are closely and appropriately woven into the year's liturgical calendar, and each member of the congregation receives an attractively produced leaflet detailing the annual programme of study sessions, social events and major festivals. This sends a clear signal to all that the programme is an integrated and essential part of the congregation's life.

2   Just as the process is not a 'quick fix', neither is it a 'cheap option', as some have thought. On the contrary, it has proved to be extremely resource-hungry in terms of the provision of both teaching personnel and materials, and the congregation's geographically remote situation has naturally meant that travel costs have been high. With this in mind, Local Collaborative Ministry has begun training a raft of 70 theological facilitators who would be able to deliver similar programmes more locally across the province, while working creatively to develop ecumenical sharing and the use of online resources . Having said this, it should be noted that those who have made the trip to the islands to deliver sessions

have themselves been energized by the experience of engaging in theological education with such a lively congregational group, and have returned fired by – and eager to spread – the collaborative vision.

3   The drawing upon wider resources from the Diocese of Aberdeen and Orkney and from the province as a whole has meant that, far from the rampant individualism of 'a congregation going it alone' that many feared, the people of St Magnus feel connected to the wider Church as never before. A vital factor since the inception of the programme has been the unflagging support of the diocesan bishop and his Mission Committee; while the initiatives have come 'from below', they would not have prospered in the way they have without this 'top-down' support, a necessary interaction between local and diocesan Church to bear in mind when setting up similar projects elsewhere.

4   A frequently discussed fear is that in some way Vestries will be disenfranchized and lawlessness erupt. The St Magnus experience testifies to the complete opposite. The setting up of the Mission Co-ordinating Group has freed the Vestry to concentrate properly upon the matters of buildings, finance and fundraising without getting bogged down in the minutiae of every aspect of the congregation's life, while maintaining its constitutional oversight ministry of the whole. What emerges is a healthier and more efficient system of governance, but one in keeping with the canons of our church.

5   It has become clear that while it is possible to effect significant change in paradigms of ministry on the ground, such *community* transformation, to use Kevin Thew Forrester's terms,[15] must be matched by *systemic* change in the wider Church; in the case of our province, this would involve, *inter alia*, changes to the way in which stipendiary incumbents are trained for the collaborative Church of the future and procedural changes to synods and diocesan committees to enable more effective lay participation. In Chapter 3, Tim Morris describes effective systemic change centred on the context and role of the congregation as a whole. This is a primary consideration when considering the vocation of a candidate for locally ordained ministry within a Local Collaborative Ministry congregation.

Conclusion

Assessing and evaluating a process when standing so close to it is difficult. What emerges clearly, however, is the aptitude of a whole congregation to engage with a sustained and developing process of growth and education. Such a way of being contains within it the possibility for participation of different kinds. It recognizes the equal but different place of everyone. It does not create elites, or limit possibility. It works hard to keep its feet on the ground and value the contribution of all. It reveals more clearly that the ministry of Christ is not merely received, but active in all, for the life of the world.

Notes

1 Joan Sandison, *The Scottish Episcopalian*, November 2003, p. 8.
2 See also pp. 38–9.
3 Magali Sarfatti Larson in Ched Myers, 'Between the seminary, the sanctuary and the streets', *Ministerial Formation*, July 2001, p. 49.
4 William Countryman, *Living on the Border of the Holy*, Harrisburg, PA: Morehouse Publishing, 1999, p. 90.
5 'We all ought to be aware of the rights that each baptised person has to being instructed, educated and supported in the faith and the Christian life': *Christifideles Laici* (1987) quoted in *The Priority of Adult Formation*, London: Catholic Bishops' Conference of England and Wales, 2000, p. 14.
6 Anglican Primates, 'Report of the working party on theological education', Kanuga, 13 April 2002, pp. 24 and 3.
7 Archbishops' Council, *Formation for Ministry within a Learning Church: The Structure and Funding of Ordination Training*, London: Church House Publishing, 2003, p. 26.
8 Archbishops' Council, *Formation for Ministry*, pp. 7 and 27.
9 See particularly Working Group of the Board of Education, *Called to New Life: The World of Lay Discipleship*, London: Church House Publishing, 2000, passim.
10 Celia Hahn, 'Where in the world is the Church?' in Verna Dozier (ed.), *The Calling of the Laity*, Herndon, VA: Alban Institute Publications, 1988, p. 89.
11 Another helpful tool in the valuation process has proved to be that of 'appreciative enquiry': see Dennis Campbell, *Congregations as Learning Communities*, Herndon, VA: Alban Institute Publications, 2000, and Sue Annis Hammond, *The Thin Book of Appreciative Enquiry*, Bend, OR: Thin Book Publishing, 1996.
12 See Peter Senge, *The Fifth Discipline*, New York: Doubleday, 1990, p. 3, and Peter Jarvis, 'The Church and the learning society', *British Journal of Theological Education*, 14(2), 2004.

13 Bishop Robin Briggs speaking to the Moray, Ross and Caithness Diocesan Conference 1999, and see also Robin Greenwood, *Transforming Church: Liberating Structures for Ministry*, London: SPCK, 2002, p. 96.

14 Home-grown material has been used hitherto, but we are currently investigating the use of the LifeCycles material from the Diocese of North Michigan which may fit the bill even better.

15 Kevin Thew Forrester, unpublished diagram, 'Ministry development – a holistic framework', based on the Four Quadrants of Ken Wilber.

3

Local Ministry development in Scotland

TIM MORRIS

The Episcopal Church in Scotland came to its present concept of Local Ministry rather late in the day. This has given us the advantage of reflecting on the many years of experience of other provinces, both learning from their mistakes and building on their successes. We offer here an account of how we are laying foundations in the early days of our own development.

Background

The Episcopal Church is a small, non-established, minority church in a predominantly Presbyterian and Roman Catholic country where history wields a strong influence. With roots in the Celtic Church, it struggled for existence during the years of the Reformation and was persecuted in the eighteenth century, until the surviving remnant could be described as 'the shadow of a shade' (Sir Walter Scott). The congregations that survived this century of marginalization tended to be scattered throughout the country, in small towns rather than villages, often owing their allegiance to the local landowning (and English-educated) lairds. The revival of the Episcopal Church during the following years owed a great deal to the influence of the Oxford movement, including the construction of many Victorian church buildings. As a result we remain today predominantly catholic in theological tradition and eucharistic in liturgical practice. Changes in social structures mean that many of our wealthy patrons have departed and in a context where local congregations are required totally to fund stipendiary clergy (including the provision of housing), the shortage of finance in the last half-century has precipitated a major crisis.

Non-stipendiary ministry

The first attempt to meet this crisis was in the 1960s through the establishment of a non-stipendiary priesthood. Each of the seven dioceses approached this task in its own way with little provincial guidance and control. This fundamentally 'local' approach had great merits. It freed bishops to respond effectively to particular needs and contexts, often with a particular focus on workplace ministry. Those ordained in this way were originally perceived as members of a ministry team, always working within a local congregation alongside a stipendiary rector. However, over time four unforeseen consequences arose.

First, the formation of non-stipendiary priests tended to take place in numerically strong congregations that offered little opportunity for the exercise of more liturgical ministry. Second, as a result, they often moved or were moved by their bishops away from their local congregational and team base, sometimes being placed in a traditional leadership position in another church. Third, as congregational activity became more demanding, they tended to focus on the church's own life rather than workplace ministry. Finally, discrepancies between diocesan training programmes became acute as non-stipendiary clergy became free to seek positions throughout the province.

Nevertheless, the contribution to the Scottish Episcopal Church (SEC) of non-stipendiary ministry has been huge and important lessons have been learned. The most significant is that any valid and permanent local ordained ministry must start from and be rooted in congregational development, never becoming a substitute for the development of all God's people.

This intentional focus on congregational development has been central to the growth of Local Collaborative Ministry (LCM) in Scotland over the last decade. We sought to avoid focusing on Ordained Local Ministry which, as the Provincial Director of Ordinands wrote, 'is a caveat, a side show to the main Local Collaborative Ministry scheme'.[1]

Our story

Our development of Local Ministry in its present form can be traced back to a number of roots. The General Synod's Rural Commission report (1995) argues that 'every congregation and community should be encouraged to supply its own viable ministry',[2] while 'Local congregations need to be helped to see that within their own membership there are the resources adequately to run a church and to promote its life, work and mission.'[3] The report constantly emphasizes how congregations need to resource their own life, with renewed roles for stipendiary clergy and everyone within the overall perspective of mission to the local community.

Approving this report, General Synod (1996) authorized the two most rural dioceses – Argyll and the Isles and Moray, Ross and Caithness – to experiment with forms of ministry that could begin to reflect this local emphasis. So the bishops introduced the notion and practice of Total Ministry, adapting to local contexts concepts and models borrowed from the Dioceses of Nevada and Northern Michigan (USA). Supported by a newly appointed Local Ministry Developer, a number of congregations in the Diocese of Moray, Ross and Caithness began to explore Local Ministry, to be further resourced by a diocesan lay training scheme and conferences.

Released to spend a sabbatical term in the Dioceses of Nevada and Eastern Oregon (USA) and in six dioceses in New Zealand, I studied the principles of Total/Shared/Mutual Ministry. Through conversations with congregational members, clergy, ministry commissions and bishops, in a range of contexts from scattered rural Otago in the Diocese of Dunedin to downtown Las Vegas, I soon became convinced that this way of being Church and doing mission had much to offer the Episcopal Church in Scotland. My sabbatical report was distributed widely and accepted by the College of Bishops who commissioned me to share its message throughout the Church. In 1997 and 1998 Mutual Ministry grew in momentum as General Synod and the College of Bishops discussed new patterns of ministry. In the year following, recognizing the need for further preparatory groundwork, the bishops granted me a six-month part-time secondment to enable the Church to explore further the 'good news story' emerging within possibilities for Local Ministry.

Mission 21

Simultaneously, the SEC was undertaking a fundamental re-examination of its life entitled 'Mission 21'. Under the leadership of the Primus, Richard Holloway, the College of Bishops invited an Alban

Institute consultant to assist the discernment of our vocation for the twenty-first century. The first stage of this process of mission was a programme entitled 'Making your church more inviting' (MYCMI) which many of the congregations in the larger dioceses undertook, supported by a trained facilitator. For some of them it was the first time that they had undertaken such a systematic examination of their corporate life, worship and mission. Although the results were not often dramatic, the very act of engaging in the process proved a turning point for many people as they began to see their part in and accept responsibility for their own congregation.

The heart of LCM

The interweaving of the themes of mission with Local Shared Ministry led to a very distinctive approach to Local Ministry in Scotland. First, because of the influence of Mission 21, mission is understood as being at the heart of any ministry development. The 2003 General Synod paper 'The next steps in the home mission of the Scottish Episcopal Church – the journey of the baptised' in its theological introduction quotes the now very familiar aphorism, 'The Church of God . . . does not have a mission but the God of mission has a Church.'[4] The paper explores this concept in terms of the ministry of all the baptized people of God, with an aim 'to help and encourage every baptised Christian to be effective in witness and mission', and also of congregations discerning their corporate vocation, 'the implementation of their own mission aims'. Consequently, we are very clear that whatever happens within congregations – for example, the calling and authorizing of various ministries – is only a means to the end of participating in God's mission and that the purpose of Local Ministry is not to prop up a declining church structure.

Second, the local congregation is understood as the basic unit out of which mission arises. The fostering of a strong, healthy congregational life offers the right springboard for ministry development.

Third, to this intentional focus on the congregation we have added two essential principles from Total Ministry – those of local formation and collaboration. Wherever it is possible, resources for Christian education and training are delivered in a local context, being custommade for that congregation, and available to everyone. Often work is done on a Sunday morning either during or immediately after a service, so that all the baptized are being formed in their individual ministries and corporate ministry together. This provides the foundation for collaboration, as people discover and exercise their gifts alongside one another without the shadow of competitiveness or hierarchy. In most congregations where Local Ministry is being explored in this way, formal ministry support groups or teams have not yet been established. We are convinced that it is better to lay these foundations properly to avoid becoming too focused on church-centred and particularly ordained ministries.

Structural changes

At the same time as these mission- and congregational-focused Local Ministry developments were taking place, a number of parallel changes in the structures of our Church made the climate considerably more favourable. Notably, the provision of theological education was radically overhauled with the establishing of the Theological Institute of the Scottish Episcopal Church (TISEC, 1993). The heart of this was a dispersed system of part-time training, open to laity and potential ordinands alike. Tutorial groups were established throughout Scotland, led often by stipendiary clergy, and much of the theology and practice of baptismal ministry was enshrined in a new syllabus.

It is significant that many of those later involved in LCM were fired with enthusiasm for this vision of being Church while in these early years of TISEC they studied together collaboratively without undue regard to the shape of their future ministries. This would seem to suggest that the process of training and formation is often as important as content. To further promote this work, the role of a part-time Provincial Officer for Local Ministry in Scotland was created. The crucial effect of this appointment was the availability of a person whose ministry, albeit on a part-time basis, was focused on LCM development. Congregations wishing to learn about Local Ministry have been able to receive personal visits, and those already struggling with its implementation have been affirmed in their journeys. For many of the scattered and remote congregations, the arrival of LCM with the part-time officer has been perceived as the first time the central provincial Church has shown any interest in either support of or learning from the local. These small groups have been helped to feel that they really matter and that in new ways of growing they are leading the way for the whole Church.

When dealing with issues of training and formation there are considerable advantages in being a small Church. It is possible to work with each individual congregation and to design and deliver material for their particular context. Similarly, people identified and called to be ordained ministers can be treated individually with a degree of flexibility. An example was an LCM candidate for priesthood on the island of Harris, where isolation and distance meant that much conventional formational work could not be undertaken prior to ordination. The need of the local congregation required his speedy ordination but he has since then continued his ministerial training. This has been a significant reminder to the Church that formation is lifelong and is never completed.

Since the General Synod 2003 the nature of the Theological Institute has changed further. In the following year delivery of training was devolved to the seven dioceses, with TISEC acting almost entirely as a monitoring body. This allows each diocese to explore exciting new ways of training, particularly in those remote and rural areas where LCM has been introduced and where traditional methods have proved difficult to deliver. Already some dioceses are developing new Christian education programmes for all the baptized, built on collaborative approaches.

There has been a significant structural advance in recognizing the distinctive character of LCM in the area of recruitment and selection of clergy. As the first congregations developed LCM, provincial vocational policies were revised and a protocol established to ensure that the context and role of the local congregation were understood as primary factors in the testing of a vocation to ordained ministry in an LCM congregation. In practice this means that a panel of Provincial Selectors travels to the LCM location and meets with the Vestry (or whole congregation) and a possible candidate for ordination. Their decision on the individual vocation is made in the light of their assessment of both congregational and geographical context, and normally would include reference to training and formation of both congregation and candidate. Such a process is obviously demanding on resources, but in the SEC, where numbers of candidates are small, this protocol has avoided the potential conflict of having two different sets of criteria or processes for the testing of ordained vocation.

At the General Synod (2004) the provincial Ministry and Mission Boards were amalgamated to further the engagement of the Church in God's mission, shaping ministry to reflect that vocation.

Our learning

The learning as LCM has developed in the past decade can be summarized as follows.

1 We have recalled that the foundational principle of ministry lies in baptism, and in congregational life and mission. Consequently the true nature and importance of ordination has been rediscovered.

2 We have experienced a 'communication reversal', as we have learned to hear and heed the voices of small and often geographically marginal congregations. They have become the prophets, speaking out of their vulnerability and so-called weakness, challenging the more prosperous and comfortable urban congregations and modelling a new way of being Church.

3 We have realized that growth can come through the resolution of conflict, which may mean having the ability to live creatively with tensions and different perspectives. Sometimes the story of LCM seems to those of us involved as engaging in a series of arguments and debates, misunderstandings and confusions, but a readiness to address these openly and honestly has always led to substantial progress.

4 We have discovered the importance of constantly holding a balance between the ideal and the realistic. We have tried to keep before us the vision of a fully collaborative Church – as illustrated by Wesley Frensdorff's 'Dream'[5] – but to interpret it within the present practical realities of the SEC. Sometimes this has meant playing the long game rather than offering 'quick fixes' and sometimes allowing congregations to choose wrong directions as part of their learning to accept responsibility for their own life.

5 We have witnessed, in almost every congregation that has experienced LCM, an upspringing of joyfulness as people are affirmed in their baptismal ministries, enjoying learning, the discovery of new gifts and being church together. LCM has demanded much of people and congregations, but in responding to its challenge they have found – often to their surprise – new joy in being serious about their Christian vocation.

The future

LCM has grown exponentially so that now over 40 congregations throughout Scotland are engaged with it in some shape or form. Meeting future demands for effective resourcing will be a challenge in a Church with very limited central (provincial or diocesan) funds. There are challenges still to be met in respect of training and formation, especially in the areas of the recognition of prior informal learning, appropriate training pathways for OLM candidates and lifelong learning programmes for all ministry. Similarly our church – from provincial to congregational level – is only now beginning to address seriously what it will mean to be a lifelong learning community.

We will also need to press forward with further structural and canonical changes to reflect the new way of being Church that LCM represents. Most local congregations struggle with individual constitutions enshrining Victorian concepts of clerical authority. Our canons on synodical government maintain two classes of membership (clerical and lay), with numerical equality – an anomaly that has become more significant in the past five years as Diocesan Synods now form the electoral college for the choice of our bishops. These inherited church structures remain fundamentally hierarchical and at odds with the ethos of collaborative ministry – and to change them will be time-consuming and energy-sapping, and yet absolutely vital.

In the ten years since LCM was experimentally introduced, sometimes developments have seemed slow as we have tried to lay substantial foundations. There have been a number of setbacks even as we have done so and there is still a real feeling of vulnerability in what are early days. In Scotland we have received much encouragement from both visiting and receiving visitors from other provinces more experienced in Local Ministry. We tell our stories, learn from one another and move forward, and I hope that this sharing of our history will assist that exchange.

Notes

1 K. Pearson, *TISEC News*, Advent 2002.
2 Scottish Episcopal Rural Commission, 'Ministry and worship in rural areas', General Synod of the Episcopal Church of Scotland, 1995, pp. 15–17.
3 Scottish Episcopal Rural Commission, 'Ministry and worship in rural areas', p. 16.

4 T. Dearborn, *Beyond Duty: A Passion for Christ, a Heart for Mission*, Lafayette Hill, PA: Marc Publishing, 1998.
5 Wesley Frensdorff, 'The Dream' in J. Borgeson and L. Wilson (eds), *Essays in Memory of Wesley Frensdorff*, Arvada, CO: Jethro Publications, 1990, p. 1. See also page 70.

4

Creating a hospitable environment for Mutual Ministry

TOM RAY AND JIM KELSEY

When Tom Ray was elected Bishop of Northern Michigan, he had been rector of a good-sized parish (St Luke's, Evanston in Illinois) in a good-sized diocese (Chicago). When he and his family drove north to begin this new episcopal ministry, it was with certain assumptions. Among these was his conviction that the main task of a good bishop is effective deployment. Specifically, he believed that if you could match the right priest with the right parish, this business of the episcopate would be a piece of cake. It did not take long for him to be disabused of this assumption.

Waiting for him on his desk in his office was a curious letter, sent actually to his predecessor who had left it behind for whoever might next inhabit his chair. The letter had been written by an older and revered member of a small congregation, St Stephen's Church in DeTour Village. This was one of any number of congregations in the small, rural Diocese of Northern Michigan which had no resident vicar, and no funds to support one. This tiny worshipping community was dependent upon visiting 'supply' priests, who would often be few and far between in that part of the world. This little congregation would sometimes go for up to three months without celebrating Holy Eucharist. The people of God were being malnourished.

In the letter, the warden observed how difficult it was to find supply clergy to travel to their church and a neighbouring congregation about 25 miles away, St Matthias Church in Pickford. She suggested that the faithful lay reader who had served them so generously for 15 years might be 'licensed' (her word) to give both congregations communion. Following her signature on the first page were the signatures of all the other members of St Stephen's. On the reverse side were the signatures of all the members of St Matthias, endorsing this request. This seemed a bona fide call! But it was not the sort of approach commonly embraced in the Episcopal Church, and it hardly matched the assumptions Tom had brought with him, that deployment of competent, professional, seminary-trained clergy was at the heart of good bishoping.

It was clear to Tom that this problem, which turned out to be quite typical of circumstances throughout the diocese, would require significant deliberation by the key leaders of the diocese. He quickly learned, in fact, that there was a history in the diocese of a previous attempt to develop local ordained ministry models, but the first time around it had been a scheme of the bishop and had failed in large part for lack of support by the wider diocesan family.

So, Tom convened a series of 18 monthly meetings of key diocesan leadership groups – the Standing Committee, the Commission on Ministry, and the bishop – to discuss how this development of local ordained ministry might be a solution to the deployment and financial problems they faced.

They acknowledged that the lay reader endorsed by the two congregations was a 75-year-old certified public accountant. What a brilliant bureaucratic solution! Ordain him locally. If it did not work out, his advanced age would before very long erase the indiscretion. By the time these groups had worked out all the issues that needed to be addressed, such as procedures for formation, for consent by neighbouring dioceses as the canons required, and so on, the faithful old lay reader had died. Tom then travelled to St Matthias Church to discuss their future. What he found was totally unexpected.

This lay pastor had modelled himself after the clergy in the diocese he had known, loved and respected. Then, out of his generosity and self-sacrifice, he had so over-functioned that upon his death no one left in the congregation even knew how to open the church building. He had lovingly incapacitated the other adults in that community. He had done all the reading, praying, visiting, accounting, everything. Clearly, what was needed was more than effective deployment of clergy, professional, local or otherwise. It was most important for the local competence of the congregation to be nurtured and developed. The seeds for what became Mutual Ministry had been planted.

Indeed, over the years that followed, these same key diocesan leadership groups, along with others, continued to gather for the purpose of developing a strategic plan, continued to learn from the experience of the several congregations in Northern Michigan, and also from other dioceses, across the country and beyond, who had been dealing with similar challenges and opportunities for ministry development. There were networks of these dioceses, such as Coalition 14, New Directions Ministries, Sindicators, the Coalition of Bishops of Small Dioceses, Appalachian Peoples Service Organization (APSO), and more. Northern Michigan both learned from and contributed towards this collaboration. The clergy and other gifted members of the diocesan leadership circle developed methods for helping congregations discern, or discover, the gifts already resident in their communities. They assembled a formation process, first designed as a regional school, and finally developed as a congregationally based approach, known as the Covenant Group process. A basic curriculum of study was authored by the seminary-trained clergy of the diocese. It took over eight years to launch the process, until finally, in 1990, the first of the Ministry Support Teams was commissioned, including the licensing of local preachers, the ordination of priests and deacons, and the commissioning of any number of ministry co-ordinators in such areas as stewardship, education, worship planning and oversight, diaconal ministry, outreach, hospitality, evangelism, and more.

In 1989, before the first commissionings took place, Jim Kelsey joined the diocese as the Ministry Development Co-ordinator. This was a significant investment, since in that tiny diocese at the time there were no full-time employees in the diocesan office other than the bishop. But it was clear that even with so few stipended clergy available to serve as rectors and vicars in the congregations around the diocese, it was of paramount importance that this overall process of ministry development be well co-ordinated.

The development of the infrastructure for the Mutual Ministry process took almost a decade, in fact. Throughout that time, the membership of the Commission on Ministry, a key strategic group, remained quite constant. It was vital that a clear vision and plan be constructed and implemented with consistency. There was also a strong emphasis placed upon consultation and communication with the wider diocesan community. The seminary-trained clergy were brought on board, and it was they who wrote the initial curriculum used to prepare the first of the Covenant Groups. Still, some of these same clergy expressed hesitancy about the changes that would inevitably affect their role, as Mutual Ministry influenced congregations and the diocese. A good deal of time and energy was spent in thinking through the implications and moving together through what did prove to be significant change. That so many collaborated in the process turned out to be one of the most important aspects of the transformation of the Diocese of Northern Michigan.

Tom Ray has described the circumstances typical in the Episcopal Church in the early 1980s as a 'painful pattern of failure'. In the conventional–traditional pattern of ministry, he observes, the clergy person was the subject of enormous expectations and responsibilities. The subtle expectation was that he or she could do things that no one else in the congregation could do. This was mutually seductive. The circle of expectations for the clergy person included liturgist, administrator, preacher, teacher, pastor, intervener in crisis, visitor in hospital and home, community leader, and then being expected to bring in the youth. What was left outside that intimidating circle? Not much; but after all, those of us on the outside of this circle are 'only lay persons' – unskilled, unprepared, inexperienced, incompetent, second rate. 'Don't expect much from us, because we don't expect much from ourselves.'

This recipe guarantees for the clergy that they will be isolated, overworked, unsupported, broken. We break clergy constantly and clergy families are often in deep trouble. This recipe guarantees for the laity that they will be underutilized, undervalued, with low self-esteem, and apologetic. 'Don't expect much from me, I'm only a lay person.' In the collapse of the ministry upon the pastor, the priest, the minister, there emerges a separation that is often adversarial – 'We–They'. Given such a discrepancy in expectations, we are assured that eventually the members of the community will be disappointed in the clergy, and eventually they will grow a bit more anti-clerical.

These distorted expectations have taken some of our most committed – the seminary-trained and ordained – and placed them at serious risk. Ordination certificates should have warning labels. The United Church of Canada has statistics showing that at any given time 18 per cent of its clergy are on stress leave. In fact, the Church says that 60 per cent have reported some conflict with their congregations. According to the national Church's specialist on clergy stress issues, 'the Church is well aware of the endemic nature of the problem and is searching for remedies'. We know we share this dilemma with other churches. For example, visitors from the Scottish Episcopal Church recently shared their concerns about the impact of stress on clergy marriages.

Immediately after his ordination as bishop, Tom Ray and his wife, Brenda, gathered together the clergy spouses (all women then) for a retreat at the diocesan conference centre. They continued this every year for some time. One spouse attending these gatherings recalls,

> Once we knew each other better we did some very helpful sharing. This constructive sharing needed to be done for our very survival. We laughed a lot over the good things in our lives, which also helped keep us going. We found that we could not say things that really bothered us about parish living to a friend and especially not to our already stressed spouses. We would plan what we wanted our next meeting to entail before parting. Tom and Brenda suggested having a friend of theirs from Evanston, a former clergy spouse and therapist, to come and guide us. Having her objective viewpoint was indeed helpful and reassuring. She joined us for many years.
>
> Even with all of this I found myself worried about the amount of stress many of us continued to experience. I could see that all of us want things to go well and we do not want to complain. Some of us had almost impossible situations to deal with at home and were desperately trying to have a happy life for our families.
>
> After several of these meetings it became clear that we also needed to meet with our spouses so we could all share what we are facing. Our bishop had Bishop David Richards (who at the time was responsible for pastoral care for our House of Bishops) lead us at a conference centre for a two-day meeting. This was only moderately successful but at least we could all see that there were issues that all of us needed to deal with as couples, not just as individuals.
>
> We had more of these annual couples' meetings in hotels. Each time another area of concern was agreed upon. A couple that had some experience with this would volunteer to address the subject at the next meeting. This was a good way for us to know each other better. We found comfort knowing that we were all dealing with similar problems. Now I realize that the paradigm of 'the minister' is impossible. One is set up for failure when one cannot possibly meet all of the expectations.
>
> This was all before Mutual Ministry came into the picture as something that would bring more intentional ministry to this diocese. As some congregations called people in their church to a variety of ministries, Covenant Groups formed to study for three years. After

members were ordained and commissioned there was a noticeable change in those churches. Gradually, as this way of ministering was accepted by more congregations, the lower stress level in these congregations was being recognized. The Ministry Support Teams were not only taking on their roles earnestly, they were also involving many more people in their congregations.

At the very end of the 1980s our Episcopal Church commissioned a national study of 'Excellence in Ministry', now called 'The Cornerstone Project'. The study provided the following conclusions:

1 There appears to be considerable confusion about the role of priests. Some priests find it hard to balance being a 'person of God' as described in the ordination vows with the heavy administrative and managerial responsibilities involved in running a parish. Others have lost their sense of call and their grounding in faith. Still others feel abandoned. Personal and family crises are common.
2 Many clergy experience isolation from their bishop as well as from other clergy and lay people. Secrecy, fear and distrust all too often enter these relationships.
3 Working relationships between many bishops and their clergy and congregations are seriously flawed.

Hartford Seminary has recently released an elaborate research project on mainline denominations funded by the Lilly Foundation. The data for the Episcopal Church has been extrapolated and the report confirms the destructive nature of the traditional–conventional model of ordained ministry. The data points out the disturbing fact that in the last five years studied, 86 per cent of Episcopal congregations had experienced significant and noticeable conflict. The top three reasons given for the conflict are (1) how decisions are made, (2) the leadership style of the rector, and (3) money.

These insights have shaped the ministry development initiatives in Northern Michigan to a significant degree. As bishops, we have been committed to address the dysfunction resulting from the traditional–conventional pattern of ministry for the seminary-trained and ordained, which was so obviously dangerous to the clerics' health and the happiness of their families. We have also been concerned to address the implications of this disease, as it has afflicted the congregations with whom the clergy are called to serve.

In the Church of England report *Faith in the Countryside* (1990) two sobering quotes, taken together, reinforce our concern for the health of congregations having clergy in the traditional–conventional pattern:

> Within the lifetime of some of the people in this place, the vicar has changed from being the person who distributed money to those who were the chief charge on the community, to now being the chief charge on the community himself![1]

> A number of parishes testified to a common experience that the life of the church was enhanced rather than diminished during a period of vacancy. One churchwarden near Bath said that 'we all slowed down again' after the arrival of the new incumbent. There is clear evidence that while rural clergy may be trained to serve a parish they may also unconsciously be restricting its growth and the potentiality of its leadership. During a vacancy congregations can often break out of patterns of deference and dependence, but when a new appointment is made these patterns reassert themselves.[2]

Both of these also characterize the experience in Northern Michigan. In a small congregation it is not uncommon for the salary and benefits of the clergy person to consume 60 to 70 per cent of the sacrificial giving of the congregation. This is another factor which is corrosive to the clergy person. When preaching eloquently on the virtue of sacrificial giving, she knows that the lion's share of that giving goes for her own support. She has become the chief charge on the community. This knowledge then further motivates the clergy person to over-function in order to justify her own compensation. We came to realize the serious danger of having a competent, self-motivated, energetic clergy person in a small congregation. In order to justify his salary and fill his time and meet the exaggerated expectations previously described, such a clergy person would over-function and steal the competence of the adult baptized members of the congregation. Such a clergy person would incapacitate the congregation, not out of any mean spirit, but out of the virtues of generosity, commitment and caring. Everyone loses, both the clergy person and the congregation.

As bishops, seeking to nurture an atmosphere hospitable to Mutual Ministry development, we have addressed these issues within a wider context of consultation and collaboration. We were aware that previous attempts in Northern Michigan to identify and form local priests had failed, in part because the plan had been primarily at the initiative and commitment of the bishop without a wider consensus throughout the diocese, and in part because the vision was still a priest-centred approach, rather than drawing upon the variety of gifted members of the wider community.

As described above, the very development of the Mutual Ministry process engaged the full circle of diocesan leadership. Each congregation which considers entering the process does so as a community. The formation process from beginning to end, including all assessments and evaluations along the way, is communal. We have learned that the best proposal has many 'fingerprints' on it, meaning that it has been shaped by as many different people in the system as possible. Not only does the proposal have a better chance of being embraced with that kind of ownership, it is also inevitably itself a superior product.

The diocese has also recognized and responded to the need to reshape its own canons to support and extend the ministry development which is now taking root in virtually every corner of Northern Michigan. Over several years, proposals for these revisions were made, discussed in any number of venues, then revised again and again to reflect the growing consensus around the diocese. What emerged is a radical and virtually unique framework for our diocesan governance. At our annual Diocesan Convention, all baptized persons are offered a seat and voice. In addition, each congregation, regardless of size, may designate up to four members to serve as voting delegates. In this, the ordained have effectively given up their automatic vote at convention. We have also abolished the distinctions between 'parishes' and 'missions', thereby honouring all-sized congregations as equal partners in our diocesan life.

What has evolved is a clear movement away from a hierarchical, top-down management style, to one which is characterized by collaboration, consensus building and circular leadership. Significant decisions are made only after consultation and deliberation by all affected parties. This begins on the local level with the Ministry Support Team in which no one person is in charge, where plans are made by collaboration, and decisions are made by consensus. Next, the diocesan Ministry Development Strategy Team brings together the Missioners and congregational leaders regularly to discuss, to reflect and to evaluate how the routine life of the congregations is playing out. Here new skills for ministry development are studied, learned and shared. Then, since Jim became bishop, a unique group simply called the Core Team has evolved. Here a selected number of ordained leaders and unordained leaders within the diocese meet regularly with the bishop to review and deliberate serious issues emerging in the diocese and reflect on the ministry of the bishop to reassure us that it is as truly collaborative as we intend. These several spheres of responsibility and accountability are often overlapping in a small diocese so that Missioners are present to the Ministry Support Team, the bishop and congregational leaders are present to the Ministry Development Strategy Team, and all are represented on the Core Team.

In visiting Northern Michigan you would also find that the canonically mandated bodies such as the Standing Committee, the Commission on Ministry, the Diocesan Council, Regional Boards and other committees and agencies pursue a similar methodology of collaboration, consensus building and circular leadership.

The formation process itself reflects our commitment to community. In the earliest years, we initiated a regional study programme that pulled participants out of their local setting to a nearby centre where they joined with leaders of other congregations for training. After a year or two, a serious and unanticipated flaw became clear through repeated evaluations. As excited as these participants were, over time they came to feel more distanced from their home congregation and, in some instances, viewed by local friends with some suspicion. By taking a select few from their base community and taking them somewhere else to a diocesan or regional centre, we were unintentionally separating them and even isolating them over time. Today basic study and formation takes place within one's home congregation. Special studies may occur from time to time through seminars convened regionally or diocesan-wide, but the basic effort is locally experienced. Our formation process, called 'Life Cycles', has emerged from our own two decades of experience, and has been shaped by collaboration with other dioceses who have had similar experience: Nevada, Wyoming and some in New England, with consultation by Leader Resources, a publishing and consulting organization serving the Episcopal Church, specializing in Christian formation and leadership development resources.

A central role in all of this development has been that of Missioner. For many years in small rural dioceses such as ours, the deployment strategy was to try to simulate as closely as possible the 'one priest–one parish' model, so enshrined in our tradition since the time of George Herbert and his *Country Parson* paradigm. This often and increasingly resulted in clergy being assigned to two, three or more congregations at once, and they would find themselves driving madly between towns and villages trying to deliver ministry to those small, struggling communities. There were many collateral consequences of this strategy, including competition among the yoked congregations, and overwork and stress among the clergy and their families. As resources continued to dwindle, and as populations continued to decline, salary levels decreased as well. No wonder the typical pattern was for very short tenures of these rural vicars. No wonder it became more and more difficult to attract strong and effective clergy. No wonder the congregations themselves began to diminish and lose their vitality. No wonder it became ever more clear that this entire system was bankrupt.

Gradually, in Northern Michigan, as elsewhere across the country, a new kind of leadership role began to appear. Instead of clergy being called to serve as vicars of multiple congregations, teams of clergy (and in some cases unordained leaders) were called to serve not as ministry deliverers but as ministry *developers*. It was a different job description. Instead of ministering *to* the congregation, the Missioner supports, encourages, educates and thereby helps to transform the congregations from being communities gathered around a minister into becoming ministering communities. Through a process of visioning and planning, the congregations are shepherded through a process of discernment, formation, ordination and commissioning, so that there emerges a Ministry Support Team who serve, not as a corporate vicar, but as a group who support and develop the baptismal, daily ministry of all the members of that congregation. In this we have discovered that instead of trying to 'empower the laity' by clericalizing a team, we do better to aim at drawing a new circle of shared leadership which engages more and more from throughout the community. A central concept is that of the 'ever-widening circle', by which those engaged in leadership roles in the Church seek not to close ranks and narrow the power circle, but to draw increasing numbers of persons into the shared leadership patterns. This is how the congregation grows ever closer to the goal of a fully ministering community.

Within this context, the Missioner is neither priest-in-charge nor vicar of the congregation, but is more a companion, guide and mentor. In truth, this role is more that of an extension of the episcopate than it is a glorified regional vicar. A real partnership has emerged between the diocese and the congregations, and, in fact, among participating congregations. The diocese has been divided into regions. Each region has about six to eight worshipping communities. A team of Missioners serves them, supported by a budget supported by a proportional sharing among the congregations and a share of support from the diocesan budget (utilizing funds previously used to try to maintain some semblance of the 'one priest–one parish' model). Each region has a council, which provides support and structure to the work of the Missioners and seeks to develop partnership and collaboration among the leadership of the various congregations.

This reorientation has resulted in a number of features in the diocesan office, in the configuration of our staff, and in our style of leadership. Overall, we have moved from seeing the bishop as pastor to the pastors to finding our own place within the overall community of mutual care. Because of the size of the diocese, we are able to be quite relational, and to nurture primary relationships with key leaders throughout the various congregations. We understand the partnership of Missioners, along with the two remaining rectors, to be such that they, too, are more partners than managers. The variety of gifts are nurtured in a way which allows everyone involved to be honoured and engaged in the priestly, diaconal and apostolic work we share. We have moved from hierarchies of domination to holarchies of collaboration.

Our diocesan staff is quite small. In the office, which has been remodelled with many open doors and much glass, with all offices opening into a central common space, we have a Ministry Development Co-ordinator, a Diocesan Operations Co-ordinator and an Office Manager. Instead of having an archdeacon, we gather together the Missioners and other key persons as a seven-member Core Team, who meet regularly and communicate by phone and e-mail to share episcopal oversight. Our approach is not delegation, but collaboration.

These are some of the ways we have tried to create an environment which is hospitable to the nurturing of the ministry of the whole people of God. When Tom Ray retired, Jim Kelsey was elected and ordained bishop, and he has sought to continue this journey. Shared leadership continues to be the guiding principle, and there are new discoveries, new learnings every day. We are both blessed to have been invited into this work. The winters are long in Northern Michigan, but it is a glorious place to live and to share in the life and work of this remarkable diocese.

Notes

1 Archbishops' Commission on Rural Areas, *Faith in the Countryside*, London: Church House Publishing, 1990, p. 146.
2 Archbishops' Commission on Rural Areas, *Faith in the Countryside*, p. 145.

5

Local Ministry developments in Waimate Archdeaconry in the Diocese of Auckland, New Zealand

CHRISTOPHER HONORÉ

Local Shared Ministry (LSM) is officially a decade old in the Auckland Diocese, although exploration into providing ministry in forms that differ from the traditional parochial model go back further. Although it was at the 1995 Diocesan Synod that legislation giving shape to Local Shared Ministry was passed, our current practice has been informed by the inspirational work of Roland Allen especially as applied by the Episcopal Church of the United States of America (ECUSA) Dioceses of Nevada and Northern Michigan. That said, it is not accurate to assume that the American examples have been simply cloned or transplanted into our context.

In my contribution I offer a sketch of how we came to be where we are today, outline some of the transformational challenges we have encountered and indicate some of the ongoing questions with which we are engaging.

The journey began with the difficulty of sustaining stipendiary priestly ministry in some of our country parishes. Typically these are large areas with tiny faith communities, which in former times were ministered to by a priest travelling, sometimes long distances over difficult terrain. By the mid 1980s, for two main reasons, this model of ministry was becoming impossible to sustain. In some cases parishes in the country were unable to attract a vicar because of the unwillingness of clergy to go to places where the schools might be unsuitable and work for a spouse difficult or impossible to obtain. In other cases, the parishes were simply no longer able to provide enough income to maintain their buildings and to cover ministry costs and mission giving. Partly this was due to the economic restructuring of our country as population patterns changed in response to changes in land use. Partly this was also due to the prolonged dependence of the Anglican Church on a single strategy for growth, that of generational increase, rather than the employment of a variety of strategies to convert, catechize and nurture believers.

Our first forays into locally provided ministry focused on the vision of 'a priest in every village', an idea borrowed from the late 1970s *minita a iwi*[1] strategy of Te Pihopatanga o Aotearoa.[2] This was applied in the mid 1980s on the Coromandel peninsula where local people had been identified, some sort of ministry discernment undertaken, and their formation begun on the basis of a monthly 24-hour training event and ongoing reading and reflection. A similar pattern was adopted in 1989 in the Waimate Archdeaconry by the visionary regional bishop, Edward Buckle, and the Bishop's Advisory Committee. This resulted in a strategy called 'Patterns for Growth', with a monthly formation programme, which met for the entire weekend once each month, employed a ministry officer on a quarter stipend and grew phenomenally from around three participants to around 17. This proved an effective way of training a number of priests and deacons. Problems arose mainly over the method of discernment. People either self-selected or were encouraged by the regional bishop. The local faith communities were not always consulted early enough in the process to ensure that the person, when ordained, would be acceptable to the local community, and their ministry received. In most cases, while the formation was of a high quality, no one was working with the faith communities to help them change their assumptions about ministry and adjust their often high expectations of their clergy. This meant that when the person was ordained both they and the community expected the person to be the sort of clergy they had always had, 'a vicar'. The people still expected to be ministered to and that the ordained person was to do ministry for them. This placed enormous pressure on 'volunteer clergy' and resulted in overtired clerics and critical communities.

It is our contention that Bishop Buckle, and a newly appointed Ministry Officer of the Northern Ministry Programme, knew about and approved of the 'Nevada Plan', but that the Northern Ministry Committee, in the main, did not see the value and wanted, quite strongly, more of what had been given from the past. So the ideal remained the ministry of 'good vicars'.

It was out of reflection on these experiences that the 1995 legislation emerged. The Northern Ministry Programme and the Diocesan Ministry Officers were the two main architects of this legislation, both of whom had seen Total Ministry on the ground in the USA and had read and reflected not only on Roland Allen, Stewart Zabriskie and the work of Wesley Frensdorff, but also had been encouraged by the work of the Roman Catholic theologian Edward Schillebeeckx. The new legislation envisaged not just priests and deacons, but a team of local leaders working in close partnership: a community of equals, some ordained but most not. The members of this team are named after congregational education on their context, their gifts, ministry needs and their mission, and people are named for ministry at a service of worship by written ballot. The names are then collated and the bishop consulted by phone for permission to approach the people named most strongly for each ministry. They are then told that their congregation has named them for a certain ministry and asked to pray about whether they can accept this as a call from God, and so begin formation.

Once this process is completed, the Vestry ratifies the team and a service of commissioning of the team in training takes place, led in person by the bishop. The member of the bishop's staff who will act as their mentor and educator, the enabler, is named and welcomed at this service. The team and the congregation then begin the process of learning in practice how Local Shared Ministry challenges and changes their assumptions about Church and ministry, and in this year of exploration every effort is made to help the congregations conceive of themselves as ministering communities. Gradually such congregations cease to see themselves from a deficit position (we are too poor to have a vicar) and come to the place where they can see, perhaps for the first time, that there are many talents, spiritual gifts and skills already present in the congregation, hitherto unnoticed, unappreciated and unused.

We have had a few surprises: for example, an enabler was mentoring a new preacher who said, in passing, 'Oh, I see it says such and such in the Greek.' 'Just back up a bit – you read New Testament Greek?' 'Oh yes, it was part of my degree!' If the traditional pattern had prevailed in that faith community this skill would have lain dormant and the gift of this particular preaching voice would have been lost to the faith community. The work of the enabler is crucial in supporting the new team members, helping them to move from being a collection of individuals to becoming a team.

Essential to the health and vitality of this way of ordering church life has been the oversight and encouragement of a Diocesan Co-ordinator of Local Shared Ministry, appointed shortly after the adoption of the Local Shared Ministry Statute (1995). Charged with oversight, care of the enabler team and monitoring of all aspects of the process, the co-ordinator relieves the bishop of hands-on daily management but ensures the maintenance of a living link between the congregations and the episcope.

Following Roland Allen, the theology supporting our approach to Local Shared Ministry contains seven key elements. We believe that every local church

1 has within its own membership sufficient gifts for its life and mission;
2 is trusted with the Bible, creeds, ministry and sacraments;
3 is responsible for recognizing the spiritual gifts and needs of its members, and calling forth those members;
4 will share its message and life with neighbouring communities not yet evangelized;
5 in allowing the Holy Spirit to work on the human endowments of the community, will have leaders sufficient for its life, without over-training or importing leaders;
6 that can't do these things is not a church but a mission field;
7 needs the bishop and staff as crucial for education and support.[3]

It can be seen that we are not only interested in providing the bones of ministry to communities but we are promoting a way of re-envisioning the Church as a community charged with apostolic, priestly and diaconal ministries. The context for mission is not somewhere far away, overseas, but present within our local communities. Key to our understanding is the idea that the ordained ministry is primarily to be a sign to the faith community, a living reminder to the Church of its nature. It follows that the bishop, priests, and deacons are important, not in terms of status, but in terms of the call to the community to see itself as sent by God, to be a bridge community between God and others. We prove the integrity of that sign by the humble ministry of service in daily life, not as slavery to a past ritual, but in glad freedom serving Christ in the poor, the needy, in social action and social transformation.

The challenge is so to create a community of gospel expectation that the people who guard power and gateways may be encouraged to share power and to open the gate so that the service of Jesus Christ may be facilitated. We encourage a climate of learning and exploration so that the cadres of secret knowledge are broken down. We do this by ensuring that, as much as possible, any member of the church may attend training and education events. We deliver these locally. This strategy helps create a community of lifelong learners, and assists in the transformation of expectations about who may minister. It takes time and continual re-education for the old assumptions around ordination, as the gateway to ministry, to be replaced by the idea that at baptism we are given our vocation from God, to be disciples in ministry.

Unpacking the ministerial tasks from a single human person and re-empowering the local community to see themselves as holders of the ministry of word and sacrament is a major mind shift necessary for this way of being Church to fully take root. We have to recover from our magisterial individualism. Enablers and ministry developers need to be given space continually to pose ecclesiological questions about identity, context and the nature of mission such as, 'Who are we?' 'Who are our neighbours?' 'What are we here for?'

Our experience has been that simply posing these questions in congregational meetings, in individual formation and in preaching has its own transformative effect – not that miracles are achieved immediately, but we gradually shift churches from the mindset of poverty thinking that says, 'We don't have enough money, enough people, enough gifts,' or 'We know one another too well to trust one another with confidences.' This can be replaced by a new mind, a 'Roman' transformation if you will,[4] which believes that God is not far distant, God has gifted us with unique gifts, and these gifts and abilities are for the purpose of building the Church. The Church is not the institution, the bishop or the priest, it is not somewhere else, remote from us, like Auckland city. We are the Church, the Lord's own people, and we are called to be in mission here.

We would like to emphasize that transformation is possible. It requires much speaking of the vision, and patient listening, and it is essential to have the active assent of the local leadership. Chris

61

vividly remembers visiting in 1997 one community that was the most remote end of a preaching circuit in a large parish. He was informed quite soon that there was no way they were having Local Ministry. Priests were necessarily seminary-trained, male and did not come from this community. Actually the congregation was small, some 25 people, ruled by a matriarch who was both leader and gatekeeper. In many ways she was a remarkable woman who did much good, but she had the ability to make or break the future. The community was characterized by both a poverty mentality and some very firmly held positions. A savage internal argument was dominating the conversation about which hymnbook to sing from.

It took about 18 months of visiting, congregational meetings and patient retelling of the possibilities and benefits of Local Shared Ministry to obtain the consent of the congregational meeting. Their decision to ask the bishop for permission to explore Local Shared Ministry started a chain reaction of transformation. They called a team which included some of the best people that they could see at the time, including the matriarch and a local woman who was already a deacon and about to be priested, trained in the Northern Ministry Programme. Her ministry was affirmed and received gladly by most, if not all. Now, this same community includes Maori people as ordained team members, who regularly conduct services in both English and Maori. This has helped the local Maori people to feel that they belong, and ameliorates the strong postcolonial English character of the Pakeha (of European descent) community. This is a community that is now able to write its own liturgy and respond to crises locally or globally with initiative. This is the community whose members were among the first to open their church for prayers after September 11, 2001, recognizing that the American residents of their community would be feeling particularly vulnerable. The community still has its arguments but now at least they are able to say of themselves 'we are a ministering community'. Local Shared Ministry has enabled them to experience Church as creative and life enhancing. They still have problems maintaining a team culture, but the savage vituperation of the past has largely been eradicated from their culture.

Another of the communities from that same large seaside and rural parish willingly embraced Local Shared Ministry. During the Bishop Buckle years they had endured a long vacancy, but used the time well to create a preaching and a pastoral care team. One of their members had been ordained from the Northern Ministry programme. Now, having recently farewelled a vicar who did not really know what to do with these lay people who seemed to want to do his work, they were ready to move to another way of being Church. This is a larger congregation of around 60 in a medium-sized but growing service town. There were many people there willing to serve in ministry. The same reserves over Local Ministry were present; one woman remarked, 'When I want medical advice, I call the doctor; when I want legal advice, I will call my lawyer; when I want spiritual advice, I want a seminary-trained priest.' Ironically, several months after that remark she was overheard saying that she thought that probably LSM was better and if they were ever offered a vicar they would decline.

It is necessary in any process of change to ensure that there is provision for and care of people who do not readily embrace what is being proposed with equanimity, that there is genuine listening, by those in favour of the change, of those who find the new way difficult. We review the ministry of these congregations regularly and often ask if there are new ministries needed, or if people need to step down from a role, so the congregations develop greater discernment of gifts. It was revealing to discover that in churches which had a self-image as 'friendly', members often did not know one another's full names, and work needed to be done on developing community.

Ten years down the track we are beginning to have some urban communities seriously consider Local Shared Ministry. We now understand that LSM is not so much about plugging a gap with sacramental ministry as a genuine vocation from God. Local Shared Ministry invites us to reconsider our ecclesiology. What is the nature of the Church? How do local community and diocese relate together? We see this not as a congregational model, but as an episcopal one. Indeed, our LSM communities experience greater connection with the diocese, through the ministry of their enabler, the bishop's chaplain for LSM and the fact that they see the bishop presiding at many of their milestones: commissioning of the first team, licensing of that team, and ordination of those members called to the ministry of priests and deacons within the faith community.

As ministry enablers we meet monthly with the diocesan co-ordinator, for support, in-service education, to report on our ministry units and to take counsel with one another over challenges we face. We try to live the sort of team we want to call into being in the ministry units we serve. It is important to remind ourselves that we are in a transformative ministry, directed not only towards individuals but towards whole communities, and that we are seeking to engender the sort of christic community that looks beyond itself to mission. We try to form priests, deacons, preachers, catechists, pastoral ministers, liturgists in such a way locally that they are aware that, while the Church is local, it is also universal.

One of the chief strategies to encourage this, which has been of great benefit, is the annual Local Shared Ministry Conference. Organized by the co-ordinator, the conference has a keynote speaker and has often encouraged networking of those in similar ministries. The energy at these meetings is always high, in marked contrast to the annual licensed ministry conference, which has a much lower sense of excitement about ministry.

There are several questions that vex us. 'How do we ensure the integrity of LSM into the future?' 'How do we help those communities which have enrolled their Ministry Support Team as a sort of corporate vicar to move to the place where the ministries of all are encouraged and supported?' As faith communities contract, and many are in that process, there is a grief over the past that results in nostalgia. We have a question about how we live through that and begin to envisage a future that is wholesome, hope- and charity-filled, and is not simply cluttered up with recriminations about what we used to do and who we once were. This is the new experience of being at the edge of the society rather than in the centre, and impinges on aspects of leadership and the ministry of the Church locally. How will people know we are here? What does ministry from the margins look like?

Notes

1 Maori for 'minister of the people'.
2 The bishopric of Aotearoa.
3 David Paton, interviewed by Gerald Davis, 1983. Published in Gerald Davis, *Setting Free the Ministry of the People of God*, Cincinnati: Forward Movement, 1984.
4 Romans 12.1–3.

6

Practising the world's future: Congregational development in Christchurch, New Zealand

KEN BOOTH AND JENNY DAWSON

North New Brighton sits at the eastern end of Christchurch city, stretching back from the beach. It used to be mainly weekend and holiday cottages. The city has spread to swallow it in the suburban sprawl. It is not a context the mainline churches find easy. In the 1980s, the Anglican parish of St Andrew faced dwindling numbers, declining finances, and worship in a wooden building needing maintenance. The diocese could offer no financial help. Options canvassed included amalgamation with a neighbouring parish, trying to maintain a part-time vicar, a co-operative venture with equally struggling Methodist or Presbyterian churches, or exploration of a new form of ministry. Eventually, they chose the last.

Appointed priest-in-charge in 1991, Jenny invited the people to focus on the mission to which God might be calling them. In exploring this, they realized the necessity of valuing the ministry of all the baptized. Collaborative methods and processes were developed: people were encouraged to minister in pairs, both for support and apprenticing; confidence was fostered by regular training; and regular planning helped the people to have a sense of self-sufficiency in mission.

They are still not a large group, but they exhibit some healthy signs of being a community of faith that understands its call to enter into the purposes of God to bring all things together in Christ, to celebrate and work for that where they are. They also have a new building that community groups can use comfortably. They are one of 14 parishes in the Diocese of Christchurch (out of 72) who have adopted Local Shared Ministry. The LSM parishes illustrate one way the body of Christ can minister effectively in a changing world. It is not a model that fits all contexts, but it is here to stay, and their stories offer success and failure, gain and loss, hope and heartbreak. What follows of their stories will serve to focus the reflections in the reality of the Church's life. The story is gathered around six key themes.

Called to discipleship

One of the Ministry Support Team from North New Brighton commented once, 'Genuine Local Shared Ministry must be grounded in the radical call to be the baptized community, the body of Christ – that's the whole point.' Getting a community to accept this has turned out to be one of the critical transitions, not just in LSM settings but for the whole Church.

At the heart of LSM is the conviction that all the baptized share together in ministry, so time is needed to nurture everyone's ministry skills. Patience with the process by which people are called to ministry is critical, otherwise the penny does not drop that it is not about sharing out some jobs, but about discovering who we are as the people of God, with gifts to be made available for what God is up to. The baptized community is one that senses the mystery of being the shape of the world's future through being called together into Christ, a relationship cemented in their baptism. The wider the group actively engaged in ministry, the more connected with the local community that ministry can become.

The calling process can seem long. Despite a passion for moving ahead quickly, taking pains at this stage pays dividends, as North New Brighton can testify. A parish needs plenty of breathing space and a variety of options to consider its future pattern of ministry. Then the decision needs full endorsement from the parish if it is to proceed.

In Christchurch, a disappointment over the past decade has been the lack of looking outward, of engaging new people, in the way that an imaginative vicar often does. Rather, too often the old faithfuls continue the task of maintaining the church. The calling process has therefore recently been expanded to include identifying gifts in all people in any way associated with the church, who are then invited to contribute in their particular way. So a critical factor is working patiently till they all see that they are the world's good news. Again, reflecting on practice has enabled the system to change as required.

There is encouragement when a parish such as North New Brighton affirms its real baptismal commitment as seen in their covenant, originally written for their commissioning service in 1997:

> We the people of St Andrew's Parish covenant this day to
> affirm one another's ministries,
> seek and welcome newcomers,
> be open to the Holy Spirit among us,
> celebrate God's goodness,
> have fun together, and
> be the Body of Christ in our community.

Support

A key figure in the LSM context is the ministry enabler. Since LSM began in the early 1990s, Christchurch Diocese has insisted that each ministry unit must have an enabler appointed by the bishop. This experienced priest relates closely to the congregation but only in a part-time way and as advisor and coach rather than expert. An inherent danger in all parish ministry is congregationalism. The enabler is a key figure in helping LSM parishes remain connected to the wider Church. The enabler comes not just to endorse what is done, but as a kind of 'apostolic' visitor who asks questions the locals have forgotten to ask, or provides support when they do not know how to go about being the living body of Christ in this place. The enabler is an 'outsider', though not a stranger. All the enablers meet bi-monthly for a training day with the ministry educator and sometimes the bishop, which enhances their collegiality.

Mutuality affects the role of the bishop. In Christchurch the bishop has offered support by always being willing to meet with the local people, and by supporting them in what they are doing and showing willingness to learn from their experience. The bishop effectively gives permission for this whole way of being Church. This has been reflected in a great sense of respect for the role of the bishop. In Christchurch Diocese, many LSM people say they feel a lot more closely linked to the bishop now that contacts are not filtered through a vicar.

There are also other emerging support networks. A course for training enablers has been run nationally most years since 1996. The Ministry Support Teams from all LSM parishes hold an annual conference. It is hosted by an LSM unit in a different part of the diocese, and offers the only diocesan opportunity each year where LSM is the 'norm' and not having to justify itself. The shape of the day has remained the same: opening worship led by the locals, an inevitably lengthy time of sharing current happenings in each 'patch', then a keynote speaker (sometimes from another diocese or from overseas), and after lunch small group time for those from each ministry role to share what they are learning about ministry. LSM parishes are not left to their own devices; mutual support and diocesan encouragement are vital.

Integration with the wider Church has not been easy. Back in 1999, we (Ken and Jenny) set up a workshop called 'Something About Ordination'. One thing stands out from that event: virtually the only people who came were those involved in what was then called Total Ministry. That was worrying, because the issues of ministry, priesthood, baptism and related topics are not confined to any section of the Church. The problem remains, and LSM parishes continue to be seen by some as deviations from the norm that can be ignored.

Priests and deacons in community

It is impossible in North New Brighton to miss the collective nature of accountability. That extends to the priests and deacons; they are always seen as members of the team. Despite the fact that priests are described as being the ones 'who gather the community for Eucharist' this does not mean that they are there simply to provide the sacraments – they are able to gather the congregation because of the nature of the priestly relationship they have with them. Similarly deacons, while described as the ones who call the church into the community and commend the community to the church, are neither the people who do all the work nor even the most visible. At North New Brighton there is awareness of a qualitative difference for those called as priest or deacon from the rest of the team, but this does not put them 'over' the others. Those ordained are also acutely aware of their calling; it profoundly affects them that the community sees them in this light.

Each faith community needs those who accept apostolic responsibility for the gospel and are recognized by the universal Church. While collective responsibility rests with the Ministry Support Team, the priests have a key role. It resides in the parish's sense that these people are not simply nominated to office but are called by God to this ministry, in and for the Church – and the people have acted in partnership with God in the calling. Without in any sense being 'over' the team by virtue of their ordination, the ordained are recognized as a significant presence within the team for keeping faith with the wider Church.

What North New Brighton can teach the Church is not about the benefits of priests and deacons who are unpaid, wear no distinctive dress, work like the rest of us, and have minimal theological qualifications, but about their sense of the body of Christ and the way they share in the task of encouraging, nurturing and building up the body. It helps that there are two of each at North New Brighton. Of the priests, Lynne is a teacher and John runs a cleaning business. Neither they nor the people of North New Brighton are at risk of seeing either of them as 'the vicar'.

The very fact that there is more than one priest on the team helps avoid the idea of priest as key figure in the community of faith. In this respect the role of administrator in an LSM setting is important. It has three advantages: the priest(s) do not become the guardians of all information and interaction in the parish, the priests themselves can be free to be priests, and the community of faith can better appreciate the nature of itself as a body. Across town in Addington, there are two retired priests in the congregation: neither of them is the priest on the team, though one has another role on the team. The priest on the team is Diane, who works as a caregiver. While there is sometimes confusion about the meaning of ordination, would that the whole Church could learn about ordained ministry as part of the whole team of ministry within the body of Christ.

Learning together

Consciously, LSM people seek opportunities for learning because in their preparation and commissioning they as a congregation commit themselves to ongoing training, in which there is a high level of interest. So North New Brighton always has something on the go. Diocesan policy on LSM has been to strengthen the life of all the baptized by making all training available to everyone and not giving the ordained special training. Too often in the Church the priest is seen as virtually the sole carrier of the faith story. LSM parishes endorse the principle that learning belongs to the whole faith community and is acquired as needed.

Learning among LSM parishes is firmly anchored in an action–reflection model. A collaborative model of ministry requires an equally collaborative model of education. Good input is required, but the major benefits stem from the engagement of all participants in the reflection on an action that is rooted in real life and ministry. Wesley Frensdorff dreamed of Church being more like the crew working together on a fishing boat than the passengers on a luxury liner, drinking cocktails while others do the real work.

LSM has a head start on the rest of the Church in this theological exploration. It may have been forced on many by financial constraints, and some will always want the crew back, but in many places they discover the joy of being the crew themselves. It is a mindset before it is anything else, the realization that the Church is the community of all the baptized, the new humanity in Christ.

Models of education offer parallels to this. It can be illustrated from the series Ken is producing, 'God's Never-Ending Story'. To tell how our faith developed from Abraham to the present day in seven study segments of six sessions each is not particularly revolutionary. What is crucial, educationally, is the group discussion as a component of the exercise. Any group using the material would not simply be instructed. Rather, having read the material they were expected to engage with it and with one another in a dialogue among 'the crew'. This is another core value for the Church – it is about our mutual encouragement.

The key lesson, in Ken's view, was that he had to let groups around the country make of it what they wanted and have what conversations they wanted, without further input from him. It is built on a collaborative model of education, where 'the crew' is not simply the clergy or the leading laity, but whoever wants to participate in this journey of discovery. He needed to be sure that he will not lead them astray in what he shares about the story. Yet in no way can he tell them what to think or how to react to it. Indeed, he has found he learns from them enriching insights into how we make this journey in faith together.

God's passion for the world

Engaging with the surrounding community is never easy, regardless of the type of parish. LSM parishes do not find it any easier than any

others. Across the city from North New Brighton, St Mary's, Addington, is set in an older part of the city and one where most of the residents are on benefits and struggle to manage their lives. St Mary's
has increasingly engaged with this community, but is hampered by
the eclectic nature of the congregation. Most of those who form the
core of the parish live outside its boundaries and have been drawn
by its liturgical style and its Celtic and Taizé music. The church
suffers badly from myopia. It needs to discern carefully what God is
up to in the world, and endeavour to be there. It is encouraging in
North New Brighton to see the community using the parish buildings, and more importantly to see the faith community integrating
with the community in which it lives. North New Brighton is making deliberate attempts to reach out through the school, children and
youth work and planning and advertising services with community appeal. Addington has less attractive parish facilities, but their
connection with the community is growing. In both places it is
based on a personal engagement with local events, organizations and
people. In LSM contexts, as in all other parishes, engagement with
the local community is both rewarding and difficult.

A potential factor in this refocusing on God's mission is the diaconate. In Christchurch Diocese there are now 13 deacons (11 in LSM
parishes) and a diocesan group called the Household of Deacons
to give them support. Each LSM parish is encouraged to call at
least one deacon. It has been said that in parishes that cannot, it
may both reflect and confirm the difficulty of engaging with the
wider community.

This remains a challenge. It is a challenge that is hampered by the
Church's difficulty in determining a coherent theology of the diaconate;
it remains dominated by the concept of probation for priesthood.
The vision of a deacon as one who keeps the Church's eyes on God's
work in the world is sometimes too uncomfortable. Nor is it just about
the diaconate; the Church too easily loses sight of the world that is
the real object of God's love. Recovery of the diaconate has been
at the heart of LSM development in the Diocese of Christchurch,
expressing the principle that ordination among other things sets an
individual apart to enable the mission of the whole faith community.

Living liturgy

What we do together on Sunday conveys the sense that we have gathered around this table to affirm and celebrate the impossible unity of the human family, because that is the future God has already established, calling us onwards and urging us to invite others to come and see what we have.

LSM parishes face the same problems as any other parish in expressing on Sunday the core of what they are about. The generally small congregations in LSM contexts can produce a greater sense of community than is possible in a large building. This is a two-edged sword. It can generate an intimacy and sense of belonging, but it can also give rise to a local congregationalism that loses the sense of the whole of humanity gathered around God's table and simply maintains the routine round of services.

At North New Brighton the sense of a team is discernible. The liturgy from *A New Zealand Prayer Book* is followed – not slavishly, but the structure is carefully adhered to. The team effort that goes into thinking about the liturgy means that no one voice can dominate and dictate policy. There is a simplicity and directness about the service that trusts the liturgy to engage the people and enable their participation; they have no need to strive too hard or be too clever or put too much in.

From time to time the accusation is made that those in LSM parishes are not equipped theologically for their task. In preaching, where some scholarship is clearly needed, a case might be made. But the challenge to make connections with the gospel story faces all who preach, and LSM preachers are not necessarily better or worse than those trained more formally. Several things help: because they know they are not experts, the LSM preachers are sometimes more diligent about their biblical preparation than their supposedly more theologically literate colleagues; quite often the sermon is the result of discussion with others in the week leading up to the Sunday; and the fact that the LSMs are invariably engaged in other pursuits during the week can earth the sermon in the realities of community life.

Conclusion

Is this the shape of the Church in the future? It is certainly a shape of the Church. The LSM model is clearly here to stay. It has a confidence about its own existence and is earning the trust of the Church, albeit reluctantly in some quarters. More work needs to be done to integrate this model into the wider life of the diocese; more work needs to be done on the theology of priesthood and ordination; more work needs to be done on equipping all the people of God to read the signs of God's pathways in Scripture, history, the present and into God's future. But this model can teach the Church about being communities of faith; it can reintegrate ordained ministry into the life of the baptized community; it can encourage the Church with examples of mutual support; and it can celebrate its common life and discern the mysterious ways of God in the hearts of people in the local environment.

7

Why is Local Ministry important for a mission-shaped Church?

ADRIAN DORBER

It has been a truism in the field of architecture, at least since Le Corbusier, that form follows function. It is even more powerfully the case that the Church and its ministry need to be determined and shaped by God's mission to the world. Anglicans, despite appearances, have well-honed liturgical and rhetorical formulae for living with the changes and development that are implicit in a missionary faith. The best example can be found in the preface to the declaration of assent made by bishops at their consecration and priests at their licensing to new ministries:

> The Church of England is part of the one, holy, catholic and apostolic Church, worshipping the one true God, Father, Son and Holy Spirit. It professes the faith uniquely revealed in the Holy Scriptures and set forth in the Catholic Creeds, which *faith the Church is called upon to proclaim afresh in each generation.*[1]

This proclaiming afresh is more than repetition. Any survey of Christian history will reveal periods when there have been different readings of the tradition and widely different responses to needs and circumstances. What counts as a fruitful reading of the tradition? Perhaps the answer lies in *discernment*: the ability to read both the tradition and the signs of the times cogently, honestly, sometimes prophetically. Archbishop Rowan Williams' one-line definition of mission is beautifully apt: 'finding out what God is doing and then joining in'. To be a church in mission means doing more than evangelism (though never *less* than evangelism!). It means having a way of being that is radically focused on God and the world. It means ministering in a way that helps to incarnate the gospel by building up relationships so that community is formed. It means fostering character within the Christian community because the gifts of faith, hope and love are gospel virtues that need to be tangibly present and available in the world and constantly reinforcing the identity of the Church.[2] It means worshipping God in every possible way and struggling to name God in the tension and here-and-there-ness of human living and perception. It means also in part having the faith to improvise and to imagine.

Mission-Shaped Church[3] (the report of a Church of England working group chaired by Bishop Graham Cray) sets a brisk agenda of challenge, opportunity and missionary method. It has been eagerly received and no one can doubt its huge relevance. What I want to argue in this paper is that many of the precepts and experiences of the Local Ministry movement help to orient the Church to being a part of the *missio dei* and fundamentally provide the structure and opportunity for a more wholehearted embrace of mission as the pivotal idea in the constitution of the Church. 'Mission,' as Ruth Page put it, 'is not for God, or in place of God but with God.'[4]

The Local Ministry movement is now a pan-Anglican Communion phenomenon, and it has come into being both as a result of theologizing on the nature of Church in the contemporary world and in response to sharp practical questions posed by fewer vocations to full-time ordained ministry, finance, geography and mission to newly developed areas. There is now a respectable literature on the movement itself.[5] This paper shows how one English diocese has worked with 'Local Ministry' ideas in order to orientate itself to an explicitly missionary agenda. In doing so it has tried to distil the theological work from within Anglican and ecumenical sources on the nature of the Church and the structure of its ministry[6] in order that the 'proclaiming afresh' can take place and become a reality.

The context

The Diocese of Durham has a long history. Its origins can be traced back to the Celtic saints. Cuthbert and Bede have their mortal remains in Durham Cathedral and the heritage of sanctity and learning that the Northumbrian saints bequeathed to the Church is still treasured. Durham has been a powerhouse in many different ways: ascetic, political and economic. To understand the place means appreciating the history and spirit of the region, not least the role the Church itself has played in forging regional identity.

Most people see Durham for the first time from the train. Travelling northwards the line opens out onto a viaduct that gives a panoramic view of the cathedral and castle standing above the River Wear. It is one of the finest sights in Europe. The cathedral was designed as a power statement: God was being glorified, but through the medium of Norman post-conquest supremacy. It is a building designed to put you in your place. Its massive, powerful assertiveness is a stark contrast with human fragility. Durham's bishops were, until the 1830s, Prince Bishops. They were responsible for running the North East on behalf of the Crown and for defending a troubled border with Scotland. This fusion of power, ecclesiastical and civil, is framed by the view. It is no wonder that the cathedral is a regional icon.

In the nineteenth century, ship-building, iron, steel and coal-mining made the North East a hub of economic power. The population boom in the nineteenth century was matched by a strenuous church-building programme (often marked by keen competition with rival denominations: the Methodists in the dales and villages, the Catholics in the towns). The Church of England had a deep commitment to serving and ministering in communities that had experienced the privations, hazards and changes of early and mature industrialization. However, since the late twentieth century the region's heavy industrial base has almost entirely disappeared. The economic restructuring of the 1980s witnessed a loss not only of jobs but of old patterns of social and communal life, and with it time-honoured assumptions about belonging and aspiration. Some areas of the North East have become starkly depopulated, others are responding to regeneration initiatives. The picture is transitional and mixed.

What gives the North East's story a particular edge and sadness is the loss of a political economy that had given it national importance and local prosperity. Until the 1970s Britain's governance was largely corporatist and institutional, and during the post World War II years this pattern brought prosperity and stability to the region. The mid-twentieth-century definition of a just and satisfying democracy was that of the full-employment, highly industrialized economy backed by a generous system of health, education and welfare provision. This collectivist ideal was sharply revised by a re-emphasis of free market economics, the impact of new technologies and postmodern suspicion of grand political theories and ideals.[7] The old order in a sense guaranteed that certain kinds of dependency could be managed by professionals. Leadership was exercised by people who were competent in their field. However, once the old economy was swept away and with it the accompanying culture of work and association, the Church's response became very problematic because the social landscape had shifted. Memories of the past were strong but the new reality was very different.

Over time two responses became necessary: (1) solidarity by the Church with communities facing loss and challenge; (2) shaping patterns of church life to fit the needs of mission in a changed landscape. Thus Bishop David Jenkins' episcopate was played out in spirited opposition to the economic policies of the Thatcher Government: communities and industries under threat needed a public champion. In the longer term the Church saw the need to work for a realistic future for the region. It became part of several broad-based initiatives to build confidence and capability in local people. It was a willing if critical participant in the region's search for regeneration. The trick, though, was not to be classified by government and local authorities as part of the 'heritage' and thus become consigned to preserving the past, nor to become so activist and experimental that continuities with the past were broken and relationships with communities severed. No Church can ever ignore its most basic task of helping people bring their dependency to God. That is the task of ministry.[8] But the next necessary task of ministry is to nurture that dependency into discipleship. Christian practice becomes a considered way of handling dependency in the light of a gospel that has maturity and wisdom as one of the greatest goals of the Christian way. (The gifts of the Ascended Christ to the Church as we read of them in Ephesians 4 root the Church's vitality in a constant discovery of ministry that is inter-dependent and mutually up-building: 'the measure of the full stature of Christ', Eph. 4.13.) It thus became clear that new patterns of leadership and ministry were imperative. Enabling, facilitative, collaborative styles were needed in place of the old heroic models of yesteryear and the customary institutional patterns of lay office-holding.

Throughout the 1990s these challenges and tensions became acute. It led to a period of intense work from 1997 to 2002 by the bishop, the bishop's staff, the Board of Ministries and Training and most of the clergy and parochial church councils of the diocese. The task was to consider how the Church participated in God's mission. We had to find what structures for ministry enabled us to join in that mission faithfully and responsively in the light of the social challenges facing the region and the problems of finance, declining clergy numbers and declining congregations in the diocese.

Part of the answer was provided by a strap-line devised by the diocesan bishop, Michael Turnbull. He saw the diocese as 'holy, learning, witnessing people'. It proved a fruitful lead. The words needed filling out with local stories, experiences and interpretation but they provided a clue to the Church's identity and a spur to rediscovering its task. Mission is usually defined as having three classic elements: *kerygma* (proclamation) *koinonia* (communion and fellowship) and *diakonia* (service). Holy, learning, witnessing people was a kind of Durham 'take' on mission. It showed that all aspects of the Church's life *were* connected. God displays a 'with-us-ness' in the incarnation; that connectedness embraces all God's people and manifests itself in relationship, reconciliation and transformation in Christ. Further, this puts us in fellowship with one another and authenticates our witness in service and proclamation. Discovering this ecclesiology of communion was very significant.

Such a fundamental insight led to the adoption of a shared ministry policy for the diocese in 1999 and the creation of a diocesan scheme for Ordained Local Ministry in 2002. The precepts of the Local Ministry movement were accepted as a faithful way forward for us. These precepts can be summarized as:

- The people of God are called to ministry in baptism.
- Ministry is patterned by the relationality of God the Trinity; as God is in God's self so the Church echoes that way of being.
- Ministry and priesthood find their focus in the Eucharist.
- Ministry is rooted in the local congregation.
- Ministry is best practised within a ministry team rather than by individuals.

This shape of the Church, which is locally rooted and is actively celebrating and exploring the gifts of local people, is also one that is best fitted to participate in mission. It is one that seriously undertakes 'double listening' – to God and context. It becomes better equipped to relate its ministry to God and local people.[9]

Working with the ideas

Since 1999 Durham Diocese has pursued a vigorous policy of equipping and encouraging parishes to practise Shared Ministry. By 2005 there were 36 parishes which had been commissioned by the bishop as Shared Ministry Parishes. Each has a Ministry Development Team comprising the incumbent together with those nominated by the parish to work together to hold the parish's vision for mission and ministry. They are specifically required to develop the ministry and discipleship of the whole Church. The Durham pattern has not been to call these teams 'leadership' groups. Nor have teams been commissioned separately or apart from the congregation. The commission is for the whole Church to minister together. The bishop simply names and identifies those who are to serve on the team as part of the rite of celebrating a whole Church's desire to witness, celebrate and work as one body.

It sounds simple but the change involved has been quite radical. The Durham context is socially conservative and one of the big fears voiced by many congregations is the fear of making mistakes, getting 'it' wrong, or – worse – getting beyond perceived or assumed capabilities. Similarly, despite the clear and unambiguous charter for Shared Ministry in (of all places) the Parochial Church Council (Powers) Measure and the Church Representation Rules,[10] parochial decision-making is not always confident of its task and nature. An incumbent and parochial church council (PCC) are meant to share together in promoting the whole mission of the Church, 'pastoral, evangelistic, social and ecumenical'. This is a fine warrant, but in practice many PCCs are more comfortable with practical issues. The notion of having stewardship of mission and ministry is either evaded or conveniently left to the clergy. Taking active responsibility for these major areas required a new view of lay and clergy roles and a much more rounded and grounded ecclesiology.

There was a need for diocesan-sponsored training and consultation processes to enable parishes to explore what shared ministry entailed and how local visions of joining in God's mission could be fleshed out. Once a parish had established a Ministry Development Team there was the need for team training and formation: developing patterns of decision-making, spirituality, and for dealing with disagreement and conflict. There was also a need for some light-touch mentoring and for a practical way of staying in contact with other parishes making the same journey.

The training and support needs were met by Diocesan Officers of the Board of Ministries and Training. The Board also established an annual Ministry Development Teams day to provide a forum and a place where different ideas and suggestions for practising ministry could be explored and evaluated. Enthusiastic endorsement from the bishops and archdeacons has ensured that the training and consultation processes are respected and seen as indispensable. Teams themselves have been eager to develop their work knowing that there is a growing parochial network of clerical and lay expertise in team working and that interests and difficulties can be shared quite openly. Many of the teams have begun to undertake pastoral initiatives: setting up youth outreach projects, schemes for pastoral visiting, bereavement ministry, prayer and intercession groups, helping the congregation consider issues of faith and daily work, or getting involved in community regeneration projects. Some have been able to help hard-pressed incumbents establish proper working practices and have set up parish offices and administrative support to open up 'a proper shop window for our Church'.

Nevertheless, there are key renegotiations that have to take place in the adoption of Shared Ministry. Unless they take place, the 'edge' of Local Ministry is removed and it becomes a mere palliative. Parishes always express an anxiety about survival and this is the first question that must be explored. Local Ministry depends on two requirements: (1) capability at getting some tasks done, and (2) a basic friendliness and good-heartedness. If either of these gifts fails to be present then Shared Ministry, i.e. Local Ministry, cannot happen. But if they are present then anxieties can be softened and a congregation can begin to explore its giftedness and its opportunities.

The second negotiation that becomes essential is how clergy understand and take up their own role in a collaborative culture. This piece of reflection needs resourcing and mentoring. In Durham we have tried to encourage all clergy considering Shared Ministry to participate in a 'changing style' process: a mixture of residentials and seminars to familiarize participants both with the ideas of Local Ministry and how at an emotional and practical level that change impinges on clerical conceptions of the task of ministry. We have found that notions of leadership have had to be reinterpreted: that priests have had to become much more aware of the role they hold. Their chief task has been to facilitate styles of worship and patterns of ministry where clergy preside but actively give dimension, shape and affirmation to other people's gifts. In brief, the clerical role (especially for incumbents) is becoming more episcopal.

The third piece of negotiation that has to take place concerns how the people of God take up the role of being a priestly people. In Shared Ministry parishes we have noticed a battle for the soul of the Church of England. There are those who want to maintain a Church that had its heyday in the 1950s. Its dependability and professionalism was the pastoral bulwark of the nation. It made few demands but it was worth supporting for its absolute accessibility. It was the Church in institutional form. Ranged against this ecclesiology is a model of a Church as communion. It prizes relationship, participation, faith, action and worship. It is less bound by inheritance and social expectation but it is firmly committed to living out its vision in faithfulness to where it finds itself.

The old model of Church has nothing to fear from the new except perhaps an intensification of its faith and a refocusing of its effort. But unless the Church is aware of these different expectations and tensions a programme for Local Ministry will only bring these deep differences to light. That is why using Local Ministry methods as a way of shoring up the parochial system will only meet with limited success. Local Ministry sees all the baptized as ministers. As it takes shape in congregations it is a renewing and converting force helping a community to turn its life over to God, to struggle against sin and resist evil; 'a community that blesses and makes holy the ordinary things of creation through offering and thanksgiving'[11] discovering both its vocation in the world and a pattern of spirituality that works in the world. Discovering, too, how it needs the vitality of being congregated and the discipline of being dispersed.

Shared Ministry is a crucible. It is a very deliberate restructuring of the Church to enable it to become a community with a clear sense of mission and service. It refines the old and tries to bring forth the new.

Our experience in Durham is that this new form of ministry is a quiet revolution that makes for systemic change at every level. Its fruit is the increase in confidence and capability of all the people of God; a re-imagining and re-working of the priestly role of the ordained in the service of the common priesthood of the whole Church; an understanding that ministry is the 'how' of mission, the joining in with what God is up to; the discernment of the great text of Scripture and the sifting and testing of experience. It moves us from old settled positions into more risky and experimental terrain. But the benefits of this new edgy existence are becoming manifest in more people discovering gifts, graces and knowledge that once they would have said it was simply not their job to know.

Notes

1 Ordinal in *The Alternative Service Book*, Oxford: OUP, 1980.
2 Samuel Wells, *Improvisation: The Drama of Christian Ethics*, London: SPCK, 2004.
3 Archbishops' Council Working Party Report, *Mission-Shaped Church*, London: Church House Publishing, 2004.
4 Ruth Page, *God with Us: Synergy in the Church*, London: SCM Press, 2000, p. 145.
5 Robin Greenwood, *Practising Community*, London: SPCK, 1996; *The Ministry Team Handbook*, London: SPCK, 2000; *Transforming Church*, London: SPCK, 2002. Andrew Bowden and Michael West, *Dynamic Local Ministry*, London: Continuum, 2000. Maylanne Maybee, *All Who Minister*, Toronto: Anglican Book Centre, 2001.
6 *The Anglican/Roman Catholic International Commission Final Report*, London: SPCK/CTS, 1981; *Baptism, Eucharist and Ministry: Faith and Order Paper 11*, Geneva: World Council of Churches, 1982; *The Forgotten Trinity: Report of the BCC Study Commission on Trinitarian Doctrine Today*, London: British Council of Churches, 1989; *Eucharistic Presidency: A Theological Statement by the House of Bishops of the General Synod*, London: Church House Publishing, 1997; *Working as One Body: Report of the Archbishops' Commission on the Organisation of the Church of England*, London: Church House Publishing, 1995; *The Virginia Report: Report of the Inter-Anglican Theological and Doctrinal Commission*, London: Anglican Consultative Council, 1997, see <www.anglicancommunion.org/lambeth/reports/report1.html>; Robert Warren, *Building Missionary Congregations*, Board of Mission Occasional Paper 4, London: Church House Publishing, 1995; Robert Warren and Janet Hodgson, 'Growing Healthy Churches: A Springboard Resource', Spring-board Resource Paper 2, 2001; Faith and Order Advisory Group (FOAG), *The Theology of Ordination*, London: Church Information Office, 1976; Bishops' Conference of England and Wales, *The Sign We Give*, Chelmsford: Matthew James Publishing, 1995.

7 John Atherton, *Public Theology for Changing Times*, London: SPCK, 2000, pp. 83–90.

8 Wesley Carr, *The Priest-Like Task*, London: SPCK, 1985.

9 Bowden and West, *Dynamic Local Ministry*, p. 52.

10 *Parochial Church Council (Powers) Measure*, London: Church Information Office, 1956, Section 2.

11 Maybee, *All Who Minister*, p. 169.

8

Beyond

ROB DABORN

As British society and culture have diversified through the second half of the twentieth century, churches have increasingly discerned 'clear water' between their Christian identity and values and those of society at large. This sense of standing over against society rather than representing it, together with several decades of numerical decline, have led churches of all denominations increasingly to ask 'What is God calling us to be?' and 'What is God calling us to do?' in this place at this time.

A significant aspect of this searching is an awareness of the God-centredness of the Church's calling, neatly summarized by Tim Dearborn: 'It is not the Church of God that has a mission in the world, but the God of mission who has a Church in the world.'[1]

As churches seek to align themselves with the mission of God in an increasingly diverse and fragmented culture, new patterns of Christian life and ministry have evolved, many of them summarized as 'fresh expressions of Church' in the Church of England's report, *Mission-Shaped Church.*[2] These fresh expressions of Christian life and service reach beyond traditional patterns such as those of the Anglican parish to explore new experiences of Church that are embedded in richly varied aspects of our culture.

These churches live with the same tension as more traditional models – the challenge to be both relevant to contemporary culture and also faithful to the Christian story and the ultimate calling to *become* the people of God. This bifocal calling is similarly recognized in the Declaration of Assent made by Church of England ministers at their licensing, which states that 'The Church of England . . . professes the faith uniquely revealed in the Holy Scriptures and set forth in the catholic creeds, which faith the Church is called upon to proclaim afresh to every generation.'

The kingdom of God serves as a dynamic theological backdrop to this bifocal calling, ensuring that the focus of the Church's ministry and mission is always beyond itself and God-centred. Of this kingdom, made real in the life and ministry of Jesus, present in the world today and awaiting its final fulfilment, the Church is understood to be potentially a 'sign, instrument and foretaste'.[3] But what does this mean in concrete terms? Jürgen Moltmann, drawing on the New Testament texts, describes the kingdom, both present and future, not as a narrow theocracy but as 'the wide space in which there is no more cramping',[4] where every creature is nurtured until it achieves its true potential. This is an evocative image of flourishing, and one that is worth further exploration if fresh expressions of Church are to respond to the full challenge of what God has called them to be and to do.

Writing in Chapter 1 of this collection, Robin Greenwood has identified five 'marks' of the Church that flow from his trinitarian ecclesiology. These resonate strongly with the understanding of the kingdom of God outlined above, and provide a framework within which to review fresh expressions of Church. The purpose of this chapter is to examine three of these fresh expressions in the UK in the light of these five marks, using them to gauge their response to the bifocal challenge identified above to relate both to their cultural context and also to the Christian story and hope.

A story from Wales

The church of St Beuno's, Botwnnog, has been the centre of a remarkable experiment in developing cell church in a rural context. The church belongs to an ecumenical cluster at the western end of the Lleyn peninsula, in North Wales. Some of the churches in the cluster, like St Beuno's, belong to the Church in Wales, while others are Presbyterian, all coming under the pastoral leadership of the incumbent, the Revd Peter James. The journey began five years ago when Peter was attending a conference in England which stirred his interest in the potential of cell church. St Beuno's draws an eclectic congregation from the surrounding area and it was a natural step, after due consultation and reflection, to set up four roughly geographical cells, building on the church's previous experience in group work. There are now seven cells meeting regularly, including one for teenagers.

The development of the cell groups has been creative but untidy: some have grown and multiplied, others have struggled to survive; some have developed a breadth of Mutual Ministry while others have more in common with a traditional study group. Although the cells began on a regional basis, some members now prefer to travel to a cell that meets at a time and day to suit their schedule. By contrast, the cell at Llaniestyn church, the neighbouring village to Botwnnog, has evolved from the small local congregation and become an important focus of its life.

There are about the same number of people meeting in cell groups as in the regular Sunday congregation at St Beuno's, but again the edges are not tidy: as might be expected, there are some in the main congregation who do not belong to cell groups, while for others cell is their main and sometimes only experience of Christian community. Overall, however, a significantly high proportion of the Sunday congregation are also committed to cell groups, making them a central feature in the worship and fellowship at St Beuno's.

The groups are generally committed to the pattern of 'four Ws' common to many cell churches: welcome, worship, Word and witness. Most of the group members relate both to the 'small church' experience of their cell and also to the 'big church' experience of the Sunday congregation – or 'flying as a two-winged church', as it is sometimes described. The groups are also committed to the principle of 'belonging before believing': by serving as a welcoming point of entry into the Christian Church, with a low commitment threshold, the cell groups have been a means whereby some have been able to explore faith and discipleship and eventually to make their own commitment to Christ.

As well as being a means of faith sharing, the cell groups have proved to be an effective way of developing leadership skills and confidence, as well as, at their best, providing significant depth in pastoral care, fellowship and learning. Peter James accepts that an improved oversight structure is needed, to provide support and direction to the cell leaders. This, however, is only symptomatic of the cell groups being a 'work in progress': Peter stresses that one of the important things they have learned is that constant fluidity and development are to be accepted and welcomed.

There is no doubt that the development of cell groups has enriched the life of the Church in and around Botwnnog: where they have fulfilled their potential, the cells have become communities where people have been able to grow in faith, discover their ministerial gifts and care for and support each other in greater depth than more traditional paradigms of ministry might allow. There are significant points of resonance here with Robin Greenwood's five 'marks' of Church: in particular, the cell groups have served as communities of love, authenticity and learning, as well as offering a visionary hint of how a new expression of Church can work effectively in a rural context.

A story from Scotland

The Coracle Trust,[5] based in Edinburgh, provides people, especially young adults, with a context within which to learn and to explore the meaning of Christian life in the everyday world. Rather than serve as a complete expression of Church, Coracle supports its members in their commitment to their local churches, working ecumenically to provide a meeting place for learning, spiritual direction, training and social events.

The trust was founded by Kenny and Bridget Macaulay, both ordained ministers in the Scottish Episcopal Church, to support and nurture young Christian adults through an important period of transition. While there is much on offer for students in local churches, there is little for those in the 20 to 40 age range, many of whom are setting up in new places of work and worship, establishing long-term relationships and beginning to settle into family life. Often they are facing big questions about values, lifestyles and the relevance of faith in the daily round of life.

In this context, the Celtic boat, the coracle, serves as a symbol of journeying, a fundamental metaphor of Christian faith. It is a reminder of vulnerable trust, recalling the stories of Brendan and Columba who risked all to carry a message of grace. The coracle is symbolic, too, of an ability to respond to the environment and prevailing weather – learning to read the culture of our time and act wisely within it. It evokes, as well, a radical commitment and simplicity, following the teaching of Christ in the whole of life.

In working out their vision, Coracle is committed to ministry that

- builds community;
- resources individuals and churches;

- offers hospitality;
- fosters action in the wider community;
- nurtures spiritual companionship.

At present, the Trust is facilitating a number of initiatives that address this commitment, including a Motherhood and Theology group, offering discussion and parenting support; and Faith and Action Edinburgh, which seeks study and practical engagement with social, environmental, trade and consumer issues. Through this developing ministry and common life, Coracle seeks to respond to the call both to critique culture and also to discern and work with God's creative Spirit within it.

A story from England

Church Without Walls (CWW) describes the Network Church that is emerging in Stoke-on-Trent to connect with those in their twenties and thirties who are not being reached by traditional models of Church. The Bishop of Stafford licensed an ordained minister, Gordon Crowther, in 2003 as 'Church Planter–Mission Priest for Stoke-on-Trent and Newcastle-under-Lyme'. The post was advertised as 'a missionary to young adults' who would 'plant a new kind of Church, evangelizing the networks of unchurched young adults who live, work, play sport or who club and pub' in the Potteries. A small group developed, meeting weekly at the Crowthers' home and based upon the four 'Ws' of Cell Church, with an emphasis on 'welcome' – getting to know each other's stories, eating together and then experimenting with 'worship'. The 'Word' was a distilling of the model of Jesus in the Scriptures to values upon which to develop an authentic and distinctive community, centred upon Jesus and engaging with the worlds in which the group live. The 'works' took the form of the group keeping their daily contexts before each other in prayer and in reflecting on what following Jesus means in specific situations.

Gatherings moved to Sunday afternoons and the group ran an Alpha course in 'Fusion', a pub and music venue in the city centre. In January 2005, when numbers made it too uncomfortable in a home, the group moved into Fusion for a weekly gathering on Sunday afternoons. While trying not to revert to known church models, they celebrate the Eucharist, sing in worship and pray as well as study Scripture.

The style of 'worshipping missional community' is organic rather than organized, based, as it is, on God the Trinity with values that include reaching out towards and identifying with each other (incarnation); accepting each other as having intrinsic value under God, yet also as all sinners in need of forgiveness and transformation; and, as fellow participants in God's purpose of reconciliation in Jesus Christ, dependent on the empowering presence of the Holy Spirit.

Recognizing that human beings develop in different relational groupings, Church Without Walls is developing a pattern of intimacy and accountability in small cell groups, each centred on a missionary passion in the leaders. 'Touched' is a cell which explores creativity and aims to connect with those who are drawn to creative expression. 'Impact' attracts those who are concerned to relate faith to their everyday life situation at work and elsewhere. One couple have also launched 'Exodus Events', a monthly music event in Fusion, which aims to reach out through contemporary Christian music and by creating a space for people of faith and none to engage with each other.

This organic cellular structure allows multiplication of leaders and expressions of gifting as well as of diversity of expression. The hope is that this structure will be more accessible to the many sub-cultures and social networks among people today and allow the gospel of Jesus Christ to be expressed in the many 'languages' of people where they are, so that they are enabled to hear, understand and respond. This structure also represents a holistic response, in the name of Christ, to the needs of young adults who live in a culture where family and community is fragmenting, materialism is found wanting, the future lacks promise and there is an aching search for 'real meaning and purpose' and 'something (or someone) to trust'.

These three expressions of Church have all been resourced by traditional paradigms, but are not ultimately dependent upon them, in the same way that good parenting is not about control but about resourcing and letting go. The centre of gravity in each of these three stories is in the kingdom of God – 'what is God doing and how can we join in?' is the implicit storyline in each case. And because the focus is upon kingdom not upon Church, these examples indicate Christian communities that are indeed wrestling with the challenge to engage effectively with both their cultural context and the Christian story and hope. A brief review of their experience in the light of Robin Greenwood's five 'marks' of Church will indicate the depth of this engagement.

A community of love: hospitality has been central to every story. Physical hospitality (an open home to meet in, home-made food, warmth, relaxation and friendship) seeks to be an icon for spiritual hospitality (spiritual food and nurture, attentiveness to different levels of need). Coracle, for example, creates a 'space of welcome' that seeks to imitate God's own life of a network of relationships springing from a love which is opened up in welcome through the incarnation. In CWW, the welcome has included a readiness to share pain, an experience which shifted the group to a closer level of community rooted in the transforming love of God in Jesus Christ. Here and in the cell groups at Botwnnog, some have been able to encounter and respond to this transforming love for the first time.

A community of authenticity: each expression of Church provides a context within which to explore a distinctive, authentic pattern for living the Christian life. In Botwnnog, the cell groups have built confidence in discipleship and drawn out gifts of ministry and leadership. The three journeys of Coracle's 'Pattern for Living' (inwards in contemplation, outwards in action and together in community) provide a framework that can be lived out individually and collectively as the community responds to the call both to critique culture and to discern and work with God's creative Spirit within it. CWW currently meets in a pub, where the owner said of them, 'You people are so real!' Authenticity also allows fragility: this is helped by the fact that CWW is small in number and material resources. Its form is organic rather than structured, and suspicious of order and set forms. In each context, the dynamic is a flow from welcome, coffee and food (engaging with each other as we are) to engaging with God in worship and Word – and so to become naturally distinctive, as Christ is present among his people.

A community of abundance: Coracle provides 'tools' to discern and live with rather than a fixed set of responses. In helping people to discover and discern God's action in their lives and how he might be calling them to live out of their faith and relationship with him, people are finding a 'wide space' of wholeness and fullness of life. This discernment and discovery is facilitated through one-to-one spiritual direction as well as the shared journey of the group. The cell groups at Botwnnog have seen the growth of Mutual Ministry, including significant depth in pastoral care and equipping for ministry in the community. CWW have deliberately not started up programmes and events, but have allowed God's creation to 'bubble up' among them. So all are engaged as they choose to be and are freed to be. For example, people are given permission and opportunity to pray using silence, drawing, modelling, writing, listening to music, looking at images, dancing, lying or kneeling. There is togetherness in diverse expression – the result is abundance.

A community of learning: in all three stories, learning is intrinsic to community. Most commonly, learning is not understood to be linear, but cyclical and transformative: an action–reflection approach means group members start with valuing their various experiences, drawing on the whole range of people represented in the group. They then seek to deepen their understanding as they reflect on what has shaped that experience. This leads to examining their experience in the light of Scripture and tradition, seeking to understand how their own story relates to and is rooted in the bigger narrative. This is taken into action in service, and as community members find themselves changed, the cycle of reflection begins again. As Peter James noted that the development of cell groups was a learning experience, 'work in progress', so Gordon Crowther identifies learning in terms of journey rather than of graduation. There is, however, also a sense of accountability in learning – not to a person, but to the values of the kingdom and the commission to engage in the mission of God.

A community of character: the Coracle community seeks to grow in characteristics that affirm the nature and reality of God's kingdom and express affinity with the mission of God. A 'round-table community', a collaborative and relational (rather than hierarchical) style of leadership, a recognition that spiritual maturity can lie in unexpected places and people, and a desire to live both a gospel of faith and a gospel of social action reflect something of the nature of the kingdom. There is evidence that God is 'breaking in' to people's lives, and then corporately God's kingdom 'breaks out' as folk carry their experience of faith into all they do. Similarly, CWW is committed to internal transformation alongside social regeneration. So, for example, the group are challenged by those of its members who are working with Sure Start, deaf children or cancer patients – each context of ministry being also an opportunity for the breaking in of the kingdom of God.

To summarize: these stories illustrate Christian communities that are seeking to engage in depth with the bifocal vocation identified above: 'Church' has evolved to relate to a distinct cultural context; and yet in all three cases there is a sense that the centre of the Church's life is *beyond* itself, in the life and mission of God.

Notes

1 T. Dearborn, *Beyond Duty: A Passion for Christ, a Heart for Mission*, Lafayette Hill, PA: Marc Publishing, 1998.
2 Archbishops' Council's Working Party Report, *Mission-Shaped Church*, London: Church House Publishing, 2004, Chapter 4.
3 Archbishops' Council's Working Party Interim Report, *The Structure and Funding of Ordination Training*, London: Church House Publishing, 2002, p. 8. Also Avery Dulles, *Models of the Church*, Dublin: Gill and Macmillan, 1976, pp. 58–70.
4 Jürgen Moltmann, *Jesus Christ for Today's World*, London: SCM Press, 1994, p. 23.
5 www.coracletrust.org.uk

9

Educating collaboratively for change

DAVID LESLIE

Bringing together past and present experience

The Church witnesses to God's creative and redemptive activity in the world.[1] It looks back to the work of Jesus and how he captured people's imagination with stories drawn from common experience. His life, death and resurrection announced the values of God's kingdom and transformed the lives of those who followed him. But it's not always easy to connect how it feels for us to be alive at the present time to the world of Jesus and a Christian tradition that extends over 2,000 years. Yet we must do a 'double-take' on the story of Jesus if we are to share the good news of what Jesus has done and make known the values of God's kingdom to a world which is, in so many respects, unlike the world he knew.

The coming together of past and present understandings of God's activity in the world means that whatever we learn about our Christian faith constantly requires interpretation and application for new situations. Fusing past and present in this way is necessary if we are to share the gospel message so that it resonates with the experience of other people. This 'double-take' on what we experience goes to the heart of educating collaboratively for change. Like a game where a ball is gently kicked backwards and forwards, we make sense of things by bringing together past and present experiences and applying them to the new situations we find ourselves in.[2]

Problems start when we treat past and present experience separately – as if each operated in a distinct realm of its own. Of course, Christianity is deeply embedded in the past through Scripture and tradition, which can make it seem so hard for us to put across the stories about Jesus and the values of God's kingdom when media images appear to provide the only continuity for our fragmented and pluralistic society.[3] Many people would say that none of the great stories of faith that belong to the world's religions can provide full explanations of the way things are. Indeed, some people are glad to turn their backs on what they regard as baggage from a former age and are very much aware of how religious zeal can be accompanied by violence and oppression. But others are not so sure that society can continue to hold together without the values that are deeply embedded in these great stories. We may be surprised, then, to discover that we have more in common with those who take a suspicious view of how Christians make sense of things than we might imagine. In fact, those who are cautious about our claims for Jesus and his kingdom may be able to help us 'see through'[4] the way we tend to 'bottle' the freedom he has won for us within the confines of an institutional religious framework.

Working collaboratively (where all who are baptized have a share in the ministry of the Church) has the potential for making us more effective in the way we reach out to people. It helps us to identify more easily with those who don't necessarily think of themselves as Christians. It also makes it easier to see connections between the events of Jesus' life and our own experiences of fear, hurt and marginalization.

Managing 'content' and 'process'

Our understanding grows as we reconstruct the blocks of learning that previously made sense to us in the light of new experiences.[5] This marks the start of a lifelong learning journey where we are challenged to question our previously acquired assumptions and then move on.[6] But the way we change never takes place in a vacuum. As well as our personal reflections on what we learn, we find that our learning is sharpened and tested by sharing our knowledge with others. It is unhelpful to separate our personal study from what we learn alongside others.

Personal study is often branded 'content' while what we learn in a group or team is branded 'process'. The first is about how we manage packets of information and is closely associated with the academy. The second is about how we learn from one another and is closely associated with the mechanics of how teams and groups work. It is easy to assume that 'content' is of much greater significance than 'process' and that the latter is something we can simply pick up as we go along. But it doesn't happen that way. 'Content' does not necessarily equip us with the tools for applying the information we have learnt to the task in hand and 'process' may fail to temper our strong feelings about an issue by allowing us to neglect the facts that provide our argument with a firm foundation. We need both!

Collaboration and the Church

When it comes to ministerial training we find that most of it is geared to personal study and provides little opportunity for consistent exposure to group learning. The dominant clerical culture of the Church that provides its trainees with an apprenticeship model designed to prepare each candidate for taking possession of a parish is hard to dislodge. But the exercise of a proper professionalism for Local Ministry in the twenty-first century must include the development of non-directive leadership skills for the clergy. Various reports from the Ministry Division in recent years promote a culture of inclusion where candidates for ordination are not trained separately from lay people wanting to equip themselves for ministry. The recently revised selection criteria for accredited ministry underline the essentially co-operative task of leadership where candidates for ministry must show that they have the capacity to enable others and work well in a team.[7]

Team training in Liverpool

When, back in the 1980s, the Church of England Diocese of Liverpool set up shared ministry teams for urban areas with high levels of deprivation (the Group for Urban Ministry and Leadership – GUML) and then extended the idea to other parishes (Shared Ministry Teams – SMT), we found ourselves on a steep learning curve. Many members of the teams found it extremely hard to learn together despite taking part in a team development process extending over two years. Some problems were created by incumbents unwilling to 'let go' a number of tasks that they regarded as theirs. Heading up a particular task would be 'delegated' at the discretion of the incumbent rather than 'shared' on the understanding that what mattered most was that all the members of the team, including the incumbent, would identify the person best qualified to take the lead.[8] But, more fundamentally, the teams wanted their external facilitators to tell them what to do. Working out how to share power and leadership generated a great deal of conflict. It was only when this discomfort was squarely faced that 'the penny seemed to drop'[9] and the team could move on. When new learning is at variance with previously acquired assumptions it may be perceived as threatening. Some learners will be tempted to stay where they are or retreat to safe ground. Others will experience the resolution of the conflict as a release and so be encouraged to move on. There's no doubt that bringing personal study and group work together generates strong feelings. But these powerful experiences provide significant transitional moments on our learning journeys.[10] This is where learning really kicks in! It is a risky business and does not commend itself to those who would like to confine their learning to some kind of religious compartment separated from the remainder of their life experience or store it away for their own safe keeping.[11]

OLM training in Liverpool

In the mid 1990s Liverpool Diocese began training some members of these ministry teams for Ordained Local Ministry (OLM). The educational method used is based on the experience gained from team training and uses group work throughout. The packages of training attempt to balance traditional theological subjects (e.g. Bible, Christian belief, church history and worship) with those that reflect contemporary experience (e.g. liberation theology, faith development, social context and global issues). The participants on the course are asked to connect what they learn with their own experience and to share with one another the extent to which they have been changed by what they are learning. Each of them keeps a personal but not private journal of their learning journey in which they put down their reflections and feelings about the course as it goes along. By drawing on the insights of personal development psychology,[12] the course encourages each participant to become more aware of how they deal with deeply held views that have played a significant part in shaping their lives to this point and how they might feel threatened by new ways of looking at things. As each participant's trust in the other members of the group increases over time, so also does their resolve to think critically and apply what they have learnt for their local churches and communities.[13]

What the OLM participants had to say

But let's hear what some of the participants had to say (their names have been changed). The first set of ten participants on the course came from seven contrasting parishes around the diocese and had a variety of social and educational backgrounds. They brought a rich diversity of life experience into their learning group. Commenting on the overall educational method used for the course Megan said that she 'enjoyed the freshness of the educational approach – we are always relating faith and learning to life'. Several of them spoke of becoming more confident in themselves. Dee said, 'I can think for myself now,' and Pen had found that 'coming into close contact with those of different backgrounds and academic abilities has helped me to feel comfortable with others; barriers and fears still within me have started to break down'.

Group work rated highly for them all. Megan reckoned that 'the experience of working with the group has given me something I could not have got in any other way'. Sam said, 'Seeing things from other people's point of view has become almost a way of life for me.' But, in common with some of the other members of the group, he found that working as a group could be difficult. He 'had problems because some strongly held views were shaken'. It was 'a realization that the need to reconsider some previously fixed ideas is uncomfortable'.

Yet being encouraged to think critically generated some very positive comments. Beth said, 'I have become more tolerant and less naïve.' Pen said, 'My faith changed from being a private one to a public one.' Marian said at the end of the 'liberation theology' module that 'when we accept the system because this is the way it is, we become part of the oppression, the injustice and the diminishment'.

Why working collaboratively and thinking critically matters for ministry

Educating for change runs counter to learning that is understood as the delivery of a standardized commodity where learners are likely to find themselves in competition with one another. When education is regarded primarily as the reproduction and transmission of knowledge already neatly packaged and where learning outcomes are sharply defined in advance, learners may rate the acquisition of competencies and the accolade of accreditation above their ability to think critically. Education then becomes a means to an end and not an end in itself. But, in Christian terms, if mission determines ministry, then each learner's personal quest for knowledge needs to become part of a shared understanding of how the great stories of faith might be interpreted for new situations. When the quality of educational provision depends for its delivery on glitzy advertising and the need to channel sufficient students through the process to make the enterprise economically efficient, then the integrity of what is delivered is in danger of being compromised. Education for education's sake then forfeits its independence and can no longer offer criticism of the system that has taken it prisoner. That is why the combination of collaborative learning and critical thinking is so important.

Educating collaboratively is much more than an attempt to recapture something of the enthusiasm of early Christian communities when the Church was less centralized than it is now.[14] It is also much more than a passing fad where shared leadership hopefully leads to the expansion of Local Ministry. Essentially it boils down to the excitement experienced by a group of people who have dared to risk 'letting go' on a journey of learning that triggers a moment (or series of moments) when they can say, 'Oh, now I see!' Such moments of disclosure hold the clue to why open-ended ministerial training methods with open-ended learning outcomes[15] are crucial for building up a Church that reaches out to the world it is called to serve.

This combination of working collaboratively and thinking critically challenges the view of learning as an investment for personal gain alone where the acquisition of sufficient credentials shows we are capable of surviving a certain level of competitive rigour and have the certification to prove it. Good education, both personal and collaborative, invites us to undertake a journey that constantly challenges us to interpret and apply our knowledge to the world about us.

True and false values

If the Church is to be an effective witness to God's activity in that world, those who minister need to gain a good grasp of how a state of false consciousness can result from our failure to distinguish how things really are in themselves from how they are often presented to us. Television and advertising transmit symbolic images that can present a distorted view of reality designed to make us unsatisfied with what we are or have. They pander to our fantasies and keep at bay our suspicion that succumbing to them can never fulfil our deepest needs. If we fail to recognize this deceptive construction of reality we fall victim to a world where facts are manipulated to serve the interests of the rich and powerful. For example, where the sole aim of business is to maximize profits for shareholders, it is easy to confuse the actual value of consumer goods and services with the marked-up value they take on when they are enhanced by advertising, fashion and packaging. Popular culture and consumerism can create an illusory world that distorts our perception of the big ecological, economic and political issues that face our planet. Christian ministers need to recognize that in an unregulated market economy those who wield power can have a vested interest in shaping the selection and distribution of information made available to us by the media. This can make it hard for us to get at the truth. Instances of deception on a grand scale influence the extent to which we trust our political leaders.[16]

Educating for change

When educational programmes help us to understand that past and present interpretations of experience need to be held together, there is a good chance that we will achieve a balanced point of view and will be able to adapt our learning for our local context. When programmes provide the space for both personal and shared study we are likely to gain the necessary skills to listen and learn from others and be willing to collaborate on the task before us. When we are encouraged to become more self-aware and can resist the temptation of being drawn backwards to a safe haven when it comes to the resolution of personal conflict, then our increasing confidence will encourage us to share our ministry with others. When we are better able to see through the deceptions of the consumer society and have the courage to think for ourselves, then we can challenge those who play power games and identify the false values that so easily mesmerize us.

These educational methods can provide a framework for change. They give us an opportunity to identify those things that prevent us from realizing our personal potential for ministry. They raise uncomfortable questions about the way the Church structures its ministry, particularly with regard to how leadership and power are shared. They stress the prophetic role for ministry that was so central to the work of the great Old Testament prophets and Jesus. They encourage us to make a clear presentation of the values of God's kingdom not only through worship and congregational life but out in the world, where it matters so crucially that people are encouraged to think critically.

Certainly, without working collaboratively or thinking critically, we would be hard pressed to offer an effective witness to God's creative and redemptive activity in the world. The potential of such educational programmes for both personal and social change can be summed up by Marian's comments at the end of her course. 'If everyone could do this it would just change the Church, I think. I think we all came in with one or two colours and went out with all the colours of the rainbow. I feel that I had been walking round with a bag over my head for 50 years.'

Notes

1 In 1987 the Church of England Advisory Council for the Church's Ministry (ACCM) produced a report called *Education for the Church's Ministry*, which stated that the fundamental aim of theological education was 'to enable the student to grow in those personal qualities by which, with and through the corporate ministry of the Church, the creative and redemptive activity of God may be proclaimed and realised in the world'; *Education for the Church's Ministry: The Report of the Working Party on Assessment*, ACCM Occasional Paper No. 22, London, Church House Publishing, 1987, p. 37.

2 Hans-Georg Gadamer believed that 'the horizon of the past, out of which all human life lives and which exists in the form of tradition, is always in motion'. So 'the horizon of the present cannot be formed without the past . . . Rather, understanding is always the fusion of these horizons supposedly existing by themselves.' He said, 'understanding is always interpretation' and added 'application' as the third component of 'one unified process'. See H.-G. Gadamer, *Truth and Method*, London: Sheed and Ward, 1983, pp. 301–8.

3 Social pluralism and postmodernity raise big issues for theology and ministerial education. Regarding *metanarratives*, the great stories that have

shaped culture, see J. Lyotard, *The Postmodern Condition: A Report on Knowledge*, Manchester: Manchester University Press, 1984. For the way media shapes culture, see J.B. Thompson, *The Media and Modernity: A Social Theory of the Media*, Cambridge: Polity Press, 1995.

4 'Seeing through things' is an expression used by Michael Williams, formerly principal of the Northern Ordination Course, to describe thinking critically. It has been frequently used on the Liverpool Diocese OLM course.

5 In the 1950s George Kelly wrote about the way we think and feel about significant experiences. By creating a system of *constructs* from the events of life, each of us makes decisions on the assumption that related constructs cohere. When learners from diverse backgrounds share their experiences there is potential for change or resistance to change as their several systems of constructs encounter one another. See G.A. Kelly, *The Psychology of Personal Constructs*, New York: Norton, 1955.

6 Stephen Brookfield and Jack Mezirow draw attention to the significance of traumatic and peak experiences that irrupt, sometimes quite unexpectedly, into the routine events of our lives and trigger a reappraisal of previously held assumptions. See S.D. Brookfield, *Developing Critical Thinkers: Alternative Ways of Thinking and Acting*, Milton Keynes: Open University Press, 1987, and also J. Mezirow and associates, *Fostering Critical Reflection in Adulthood: A Guide to Transformative and Emancipatory Learning*, San Francisco: Jossey-Bass, 1990.

7 See the 2005 revision of *The Report of a Working Party on Criteria for Selection for Ministry in the Church of England*, ABM Policy Paper No. 3A, The Central Board of Finance of the Church of England: Church House Publishing, 1993; The Archbishops' Council, *Mind the Gap: Integrated Continuing Ministerial Education for the Church's Ministers*, London: Church House Publishing, 2001; The Ministry Division of the Archbishops' Council, *Formation for Ministry within a Learning Church*, London: Church House Publishing, 2002; The Ministry Division of the Archbishops' Council, *Mission and Ministry: The Churches' Validation Framework for Theological Education*, London: Church House Publishing, 2003; The Archbishops' Council, *Training for Collaboration in Ministry: Promoting Good Practice in IME (Initial Ministerial Education)*, London: Church House Publishing, 2003.

8 B. Whitehead, *Clergy/Laity Relationships in Shared Ministry in Contrasting Contexts*, Liverpool: Liverpool Diocesan Board of Ministry, 1993.

9 Ian Ramsey spoke of 'situations "coming alive", "taking on depth", situations in which "the penny drops", where "eye meets eye", and where "hearts miss a beat"'; I. Ramsey, *Christian Empiricism*, London: Sheldon Press, 1974, p. 159.

10 Robert Kegan describes a process of differentiation and reintegration when new experiences disturb a person's previously acquired equilibrium; R. Kegan, *The Evolving Self: Problem and Process in Human Development*, Cambridge, MA: Harvard University Press, 1982.

11 Paulo Freire called this 'the banking concept of education'; P. Freire, *Pedagogy of the Oppressed*, London: Penguin Books, 1972.

12 The background here is James Fowler's sequential faith development stages and the insights of psychoanalytic object relations theory, which tells how we construct our sense of self from the conflicts of separation experienced in childhood and adolescence; see J.W. Fowler, *Stages of Faith: The Psychology of Human Development and the Quest for Meaning*, San Francisco: Harper and Row, 1981; and W.W. Meissner, *Psychoanalysis and Religious Experience*, New Haven: Yale University Press, 1994.

13 An outline of transformative education may be found at Appendix 5 of *Stranger in the Wings*, ABM Policy Paper No. 8, London: Church House Publishing, 1998, pp. 122–8. See also my article on 'Transformative learning and ministerial education in the Church of England – some examples of appropriate ways of engaging the public realm in the context of late modernity', *British Journal of Theological Education*, 14(2), February 2004.

14 E. Schillebeeckx, *Ministry, a Case for Change*, London: SCM Press, 1980.

15 David Kolb warns that the vogue for defining learning in terms of outcomes is tantamount to an admission for non-learning because they prevent the modification of ideas as a result of gained experience; see D. Kolb, *Experiential Learning*, Englewood Cliffs, NJ: Prentice Hall, 1984.

16 Ways in which false consciousness distorts reality are powerfully illustrated by writers of the Frankfurt School of philosophy that flourished in the middle of the last century. But their concerns are shared by a number of present-day writers in the social sciences. When dominant political and economic interests shape ideas, they create a kind of *ideological bubble* that obscures real social relations. Thinking critically helps us stay outside the bubble, or at least recognize it for what it is; see T. Adorno and M. Horkheimer, *Dialectic of Enlightenment*, London: Verso, 1979, and D. Frisby, *Fragments of Modernity: Theories of Modernity in the Work of Simmel, Kracauer and Benjamin*, Cambridge: Polity Press, 1985. Regarding consumerism in particular, see J. Baudrillard, *The Consumer Society: Myths and Structures*, London: Sage Publications, 1998.

10

Collaboration and leadership in Welsh ordination training

PETER SEDGWICK

Decline and collaboration: two features of contemporary church life

It has become a commonplace of debate in the British churches, especially the Protestant churches, that we must recognize how steep has been the decline in recent years of church membership. There have been a whole series of books in recent years that either describe the decline,[1] suggest why churches are ill equipped to reverse the decline unless they change,[2] or offer new ways of being Church which will reverse the decline.[3] Wales has some of the steepest rates of decline, so frightening that it is very doubtful that many congregations in Wales realize how near the edge many church denominations are.[4] Insofar as the new mood in publishing represents an attempt to see this situation clearly, these books are a sign which is well and good, and one would be a fool to resist it. Nevertheless there is a danger that the importance of changing how the churches operate leads to a reliance on what has been described as new public sector management. Many civil servants have charted how from the mid 1970s onwards the old culture of the public services, with its emphasis on vocation, serving the public and responding to need, became replaced by an emphasis on efficiency.

David Faulkner is but one of many when he writes on changes in the Civil Service in the last two decades:

> There are warnings to be heeded – about the effect of a performance culture which is too internally or financially driven, of a structure of accountability which operates only in one direction or too narrow criteria, and the loss or corruption of a spirit of public service.[5]

He also writes of 'the emphasis on economy, efficiency and on value for money; on the assessment of performance through the measurement of inputs and outputs and the use of quantified indicators'.[6] This is a deeply experienced writer on the Civil Service (first a senior civil servant himself, then an academic writing about the subject) raising serious doubts about the nature of reform in government. So, by analogy, what raises concern in church life is that the use of statistical criteria for measuring success and failure seems to be ever more prevalent as the way of deciding policy. There is clearly a proper place for management, but if it is primarily about monitoring and setting outcomes many will feel disempowered.

The context of decline frequently produces the response of leadership training in the churches. Is this just a quick fix? The danger is of business-management culture being imposed on churches as has happened in public sector bodies, e.g. education, health, prisons. This section does not oppose such change. It may indeed be a good thing, but what matters is that it is not a slavish copying of the secular world.

This debate about mission, leadership and change sits alongside another about the emphasis on collaboration (and in earlier periods enabling 'lay ministry', sometimes called servant ministry). Many admirable developments have resulted but there have also been dangers of a loss of urgency in 'middle of the road' churches: a mutual acceptance by clergy and people of becoming slowly ever more marginal to mainstream society and a rather passive acceptance that the Church's norm should be the way of life of an older generation.

One sharp question that therefore needs to be asked is how dynamic leadership as envisaged by some models of ministry can be accommodated to models of collaboration. To put it even more sharply, is the talk of enabling servant ministry by laity and clergy alike in fact the talk of a past generation of theological training? The answer must be 'no', but it is important to show how the theological justification of leadership, collaboration, formation and character is presented.

The purpose of this article is twofold. One is to explore the relationship of leadership formation and collaborative ministry with each other in the context of modern Britain, especially in nations marked by the co-existence of poverty and prosperity, both of which (as I will show) affect character and formation deeply. The second purpose is to show how there can be a proper development of the tradition of Anglican theology on the Church, into a deeper understanding of collaborative ministry. The work of Robin Greenwood, especially his writings on priesthood,[7] is of course of great importance in this regard, and this article should be seen as a footnote to that literature.

Collaborative ministry begins with the centrality of the theology of baptism. As Hugh Lavery puts it:

> the symbolism of baptism is that of death and resurrection. It is a dying and rising . . . Baptism is a real change. It is a change of consciousness. The fear centred become the love centred Easter people, risen and renewed. Life is the key word in baptism.[8]

In Acts 2.14–47 Scripture specifies the result of initiation to be a Spirit-filled life, dedicated to community (*koinonia*), breaking of bread (*klasei tou artou*), prayers (*proseuchais*) and teaching (*didache*). This is a foundational ecclesiology, in which the gospel is proclaimed.

A full ecclesiology turns on three things: the Church being a living sign of God's presence in Christ through the empowerment of the Spirit; the Church being an efficacious sign, in which the Church through its sacraments and lived reality can bring to reality what it signifies; third, lest we become too cosy, the Church being a foregathering of the whole human family, in which the communion of God with humankind is first lived out. These three aspects are the inspiration also of contemporary ecclesiology, within which collaborative (or local) ministry has an important place.[9]

The study from Northern Michigan in this collection of essays (Chapter 4) remarks on 'considerable confusion about the role of priests' 20 years ago. That would be true elsewhere, with poor relationships between clergy, their peers, congregations and bishops. The answer is to empower local collaboration, to work at the building of consensus, and to see clergy as developers of congregations. The article speaks of supporting 'the baptismal, daily ministry of all the members of that congregation'. Shared leadership is the guiding principle, though there is a firm commitment to leadership. This change in the development of the role of clergy obviously has an impact on how clergy are trained. St Michael's College, which is the only theological college in Wales for the Methodist Church and the (Anglican) Church in Wales, has embraced these new changes wholeheartedly.

Peter Sedgwick

Formation and mission: the importance
of character

As colleges, courses and schemes embrace with enthusiasm this new
world of ministry development, planning missionary churches and
leadership (and, as said before, there is nothing intrinsically wrong
with this), it is worth asking how such emphases in the curriculum
require a new look at formation. This too is much under scrutiny
at the present time. It is worth beginning as an exploration of the
concept of formation with Newman's reflection on the importance
of character:

> We shall find it difficult to estimate the moral power which a single
> individual, trained to practise what he teaches, may acquire in his own
> circle, in the course of years. While the Scriptures are thrown upon
> the world, as if the common property of any who choose to appro-
> priate them, he is, in fact, the legitimate interpreter of them.[10]

Newman argues here that religious truth will only persuade those who
do not believe if they are convinced by the moral power of those who
live by its message. That is a sobering statement, given the yawning
gulf in moral belief and attitudes between most young people and
those who still go faithfully to church. Newman follows up his argument by claiming that Christian discipleship is something we only
learn by hard-won experience:

> We are to begin with loving our friends about us, and gradually to
> enlarge the circle of our affections, till it reaches all Christians, and
> then all men . . . We see then how absurd it is, when writers . . . talk
> magnificently about loving the whole human race with a comprehen-
> sive affection, of being friends of all mankind . . . this is not to love
> men, it is but to talk of love. The real love of man *must* depend on
> practice.[11]

'The real love of man *must* depend on practice.' This takes us directly
into moral formation. Such a concern must be related intimately to
virtue ethics and the shaping of character.[12] The debate about ethical
theory in recent decades has revived the Greek and Roman concern
for virtue, concentrating instead on the simple question 'How should
we live?' As Duncan Forrester has well said, 'Our understanding of
what is good and right is not commonly the end result of a process
of reasoning, but something we receive from others.'[13]

The nature of formation stems from a long theological tradition which is found in Aquinas and (more recently) in Stanley Hauerwas as they reflect on the virtues which make up our character. Even in moral reasoning itself, moral choices and actions flow out of the character of a person. The reliability of a person is crucial for how far we can trust a person to act in a particular way:

> A trait of character which is in some way praiseworthy, admirable or desirable [consists of] stable and effective dispositions to act in particular ways, as opposed to inclinations which are easily lost, or which do not consistently lead to corresponding kinds of action.[14]

One of the major reasons why this is difficult is well pointed out by Dan Hardy in his recent reflection on theological education.[15] Hardy identifies why it is so hard to achieve the formation of moral character. The 'displacement of accepted authorities in truth and morals; plurality and fragmentation of meaning systems; social fragmentation through economics and marketing; [and] isolation of the individual as one who brings coherence of meaning' lead to dilemmas in seeking to lead a life under God's purposes. The result is that

> stable, religiously based forms of life and understanding – including those of the Christian faith – have been destabilized by complex causes to the extent that 'the easiest thing is to do nothing'. This has a paralytic effect on leaders and most others . . . To do anything in such a confusing situation is more than most people can manage. To motivate people requires something strong enough to lift them from their lethargy.[16]

Hardy sees that the major task of Western theological education today is to respond to this agenda. We have to be formed in such a way that our common life is shaped by God's wisdom, truth and holiness and we have to find ways of learning that. As Hardy says, 'What kinds of theological education will develop a spiritual discipline of wisdom embedded in the Church's corporate life as it engages with the world today?' We have here an echo across nearly two centuries of Newman's sermon on character: 'the real love of man must depend on practice'.

Hardy draws on the Old Testament conforming of Israel to the wisdom of God and on the growth of Jesus in his father's business, as well as much early Christian education. All this centres on one point. Learning must be about moral formation which permeates the understanding of theology, and that embeddedness is only fully real when it is related to 'active engagement with the mission of Christ in the world'. This leads our argument one step further. The primary challenge in 'active engagement with the mission of Christ in the world' is that the cultural life of Europe in the twenty-first century is itself no longer sympathetic to the practice of Christianity. That is a bold claim to make, and the next section will substantiate it in more detail.

In this climate the decline of the churches comes as no surprise. However, what matters is that the churches engage in a collaborative manner, embodying shared leadership and vision, as illustrated in many examples of Local Ministry. The moral formation which shapes future clergy cannot be about setting them apart, but rather about seeing how leadership can be exercised collaboratively. St Michael's College would defend its pattern of mixed residential and non-residential training but only if it enables the process of collaborative learning and leadership formation to take place at the same time. The answer to the sharp question put at the beginning of this article as to whether collaborative ministry can also accommodate leadership in models of ministry is that this is what we are struggling to achieve in our training, residentially and non-residentially, in this college.

The social shaping of character: poverty, deprivation and social complexity

Duncan Forrester argues that we will always modify whatever it is in terms of social influence that we have received and what we absorb from our environment, but the crucial issue is that nevertheless we do actually absorb it.[17] The social shaping of character, identity and virtue cannot be ignored. It is not for nothing that children who grow up in the poorest estates surrounded by violence are more at risk of delinquent behaviour than others born in more settled communities. Equally, recent research shows that geographical determinants are a much greater predictor of whether a child goes to university or not than decisions about levels of debt.

> Whether school leavers go to university is almost entirely dependent on a postcode lottery which leaves people from 'good' areas six times more likely to make the leap than those from deprived areas, according to the biggest ever survey of students' backgrounds.[18]

This is not to argue for determinism because communities can be changed and individuals can transcend them. But within such communities there are always unconscious, and implicit, but nonetheless very real guidelines for what is seen to be appropriate moral behaviour. One of the most challenging features of contemporary Wales is the economic decline of many communities (especially in the valleys of South Wales) and the spread across them of patterns of addiction, vandalism and broken families in the wake of poverty. That is a travesty of 'appropriate moral behaviour', but it is wrong to condemn too quickly. There are many ways of seeking to escape the profound hopelessness of life in areas of high unemployment. Those who work as clergy and community workers there know how hard it is to sustain communities of trust and nurture, and the churches (of all denominations) have spent a great deal of effort in the last few years in responding to such deprivation.[19] But it in no way undervalues this work to say that it is very hard, and churches in such areas have continued to decline, sometimes to very small congregations.

Not every community is, of course, poor or deprived. There has been increasing affluence in Britain in recent years and there are many places where churches flourish in the midst of prosperity. Many such places can be found in Wales, especially in Cardiff, which feels in some areas to be booming. Nevertheless, once again the formation of character by the communities in which we live and work takes place for good and ill. There is much to applaud – new opportunities for women and minority groups, greater tolerance, more education – but there are warnings.

Many commentators would argue that our whole pattern of working in a late capitalist environment makes it difficult to sustain the formation of character. The praise for Richard Sennett's book *The Corrosion of Character: Personal Consequences of Work in the New Capitalism*[20] from many involved in management shows how much the effects of stress, short-term contracts and mobile communities induce a lack of belief that the formation of character is even desirable. In other words, if the churches are to emphasize formation as an essential aspect of ordination training, they do so when, from the effects of both poverty and prosperity (in very different ways), such a concept is harder to sustain. This needs to be recognized more clearly than it seems to be.

Communities can be created in many ways. A geographical community or a community at work is not the same as a community of faith, although in past centuries where Christendom was the norm they may have been hard to disentangle. However, although it is true that there are many different forms of community which should not be confused, the central point remains true. Moral formation goes on within a community. Moral action is almost never an isolated act independent of the formation within a community. To put it bluntly: it is not enough to talk about collaborative ministry in the Church if that does not take account of class, poverty, wealth distribution and opportunities for individual and social change. What matters then is how the process of economic and social change within an ordinary, everyday community can be helped or hindered by the presence of another community which is that of the church. Furthermore, within that church community it will be crucially important how its own leaders (clergy and laity alike) are formed in character and leadership. All too often this has been neglected in the past, with disastrous results.

This brings us once again to the central point of this article. *Can collaborative ministry also embody patterns of leadership, especially where congregations have been in decline for years?* This can be put more theologically. Can there be dynamic characters, formed in leadership, which personify the character of Christ but which in so doing exemplify the nature of *koinonia* (which can be translated as Spirit-filled community, or collaboration) as the essential nature of the Church? And can these individuals exemplify leadership so that deprived communities can have their own resources evoked in ways that respect those who live there? Can there be ways of speaking to people in prosperity as well, so that the corrosive effects of work can be resisted? Can there be ways of forming individuals within communities in such a way that those individuals are made more dynamic, aware of the kingdom, and open to God's promises?

If this is the case then to speak of the Church as a moral community or community of shared vision is to say much more than that the Church holds strong views (sometimes very strong, even intemperate views) about moral issues. The Church is where formation can happen for lives that reflect the values of the kingdom of God. Putting it this way implies that moral character can be seen in a dynamic way. Since the kingdom in Christian theology is always seen as in-breaking, dynamic and revealing the saving power of God in Christ, then it follows that individual and communal character that reflects the kingdom must itself be dynamic. Communal or Local Ministry must also reflect that dynamic character.

The challenge of formation and mission: implications for the curriculum

Forrester points out that moral formation is about recognizing what our destiny is.[21] Hardy speaks of developing the wisdom to constitute the Church as an agent of God's mission. That puts it well, because seeking one's destiny, or developing wisdom, is not a static concept, whatever else it may be. Patterns of motivation need to be encouraged, as we grow in the likeness of Christ. It is crucial that the insight of Ephesians 4.13 is recognized. As we grow into the full stature of Christ so we build up the body of Christ. Our individual growth contributes to the change and development of the community, which in turn shapes us as well. There is a symbiotic relationship here, a give and take that it is crucial to be aware of. What is different in Ephesians is that the community is ultimately grounded in Christ. It is also the case that Ephesians points to a shared grounding: 'some apostles, some prophets, some evangelists'. However, in all of this it is the 'building up of the body of Christ' that matters. So collaborative ministry must be dynamic, open to the world, and aware of social and political realities.

If theological training is meant to give the answer to the long decline of the churches in Britain, through training of future clergy, presently serving clergy and the laity in such activities as mission, leadership and collaborative ministry, then a huge amount rests on this. As we have argued above, this has to be further expressed through formation of character in a dynamic way. There are three areas which future training must consider in the light of this debate.[22] First, there is the issue of professionalism, collaborative leadership and core skills. Second, there is the commitment to some form of continuing residential training. The third is the nature of the curriculum, and how it can embody an integrated approach in a way that can be called 'wisdom'. The theory is that these leaders form churches as moral and collaborative communities, which can in turn transform the society around them. The pressing question is whether this theory works, or how this feedback is conveyed to colleges and courses from former students. I wish to raise each of these points in turn.

On the first point, that of core skills and professionalism, one way of conceptualizing the question of training for formation and mission is to say that training must give people core skills. This implies that those who exercise their skills can be comfortable in liturgy, pastoral care and mission whatever the circumstances. Whether it is a suburban parish or a rural one, there are core skills which can then be refined to take account of the particular circumstances. These core skills are there to build a community of love and nurture in which individuals can grow, feel secure in their growth and transform others. This is a matter of professionalism, and it is related to collaborative ministry as well.

This is both a collaborative and a leadership venture. Some members of congregations may be pretty damaged by the world, and the task of the community is to be a family for them. That requires both leadership and a drawing out of people, their talents and gifts, while providing a secure environment. Within that community there should be an ethic of selflessness, self-sacrifice and care for others. A good definition of episcope for the twenty-first century would be a combination of secular leadership and Christian wisdom that is placed in the context of a Christian community of love and nurture. It depends on the proper exercise of core skills. This is what we seek to teach at St Michael's.

On the second point, that of the future of residential training, both the bishops of the Church in Wales and the leaders of the Methodist Church in Wales have a commitment to continuing residential training. Residential training, if it is going to survive today, must enable the working out of a contextual theology in which the variety of community life informs the training of ordinands.[23] Communities are, of course, not simply residential groups, and non-residential communities also can and do form students in particular ways. St Michael's interweaves both residential and non-residential communities, here in Llandaff and by training other non-residential communities across Wales. It also trains ordinands, readers and laity together. All future training for ministry must always value both residential and non-residential options as the context for formation.

What a residential community allows is a greater sense, not of a community living by established rules, nor even simply of a community under godly discipline (to use the language of its founder over a century ago), but of living together as a varied group of individuals who seek to discern the truth of God's wisdom in that place.

The community where I work at St Michael's College, Llandaff, sought to provide 40 years ago exactly this semi-monastic type of training. They were all male Church in Wales ordinands who were unmarried or whose families did not live near the college. Today we have men and women, we are an ecumenical college of Methodists, Anglican and Reformed, and we have students from across the world. We train residentially and non-residentially, alongside each other. What does it mean to find God's wisdom in such a place with a variety of liturgies, practices and theologies? There is no easy answer to this, but equally we do not give up the attempt and say, 'Anything goes.' What we seek is a practical, lived vision of Christ in our midst. This means, then, to be fashioned into an Anglican, Methodist or other denominational theology appropriate to its time and place.

The decline over the last four decades in residential provision can be explained by a reaction against the rule-bound nature of traditional Anglican (and indeed Catholic) training. As manuals of moral and doctrinal theology were relegated to the back shelves of libraries, so a new form of training emerged. However, it is important to stress once more that this did not mean a purely relativist approach to ethics and doctrine where anything goes. Situation ethics in the 1960s (referring to the book with that title and as a movement) did the Church and theology no favours at all. The rise of contextual theology, and the awareness of historical consciousness in systematic and moral theology, needs to be held alongside the need to create an authentic theology that speaks to the community of faith about the 'wisdom' which that community hands on in its worship and learning. A properly formed integration of theology and practice which is sensitive to its context will show how a community of ministerial training (lay and ordained) is possible.

This discernment draws on Bonhoeffer's celebrated distinction between a community of desire and a community of truth.[24] Communities of truth are places where people come together not because they have common interests and enjoyments, but because they perceive themselves to be called by Christ. Community life requires that the diversity of the community must be respected and enjoyed. Much residential community life will have distance within it, which means freedom for others, allowing them to be themselves, and not imagining them as we would wish them to be. Above all, community life requires the practice of service and service means the building up of community.[25]

That community embodies what it means to be collaborative. The formation process, character and leadership turns on how staff and students alike can model how collaboration can take place. Placement in parishes, relationships with staff, and co-operation with each other in college all seek to embody that sharing of vision and mutual empowerment. However, there are also downsides to residential training. The recent document from the Ministry Division of the Church of England on the curriculum of ordination makes the point strongly that 'all ministerial education is contextual because the communities in which patterns of Christian living are being shaped crucially shape ministry'.[26]

There is no doubt that at times residential communities can become ivory towers, hot-houses, remote and precious places from where ministry of lay and ordained is carried on. The document goes on to speak of the 'raw, intractable features of human experience' in a parish where ministry will be carried on.[27] While this makes parish ministry sound rather like an epic trip to the Arctic regions, the point is well made.

Whether a community in which that training goes on is residential or not, or perhaps made up of elements of both, staff need to model an accepting community in which individuals can develop. This community can embody an ethic of selflessness and sacrifice, where leadership and wisdom can provide a true episcope for the future Church. In one way the discipline of academic study isolates students and militates against community. In another way the experience of study can involve facing up to enormous personal challenges of faith, which requires a hard-won personal maturity. This integration is again something we seek to share as a body, and to be a crucial part of training, not to be forgotten when new clergy leave this college to begin 'real ministry' where talk of collaboration can be disregarded as a passing whim of college staff.

What Bonhoeffer meant by the life of service and Newman meant by the practice of real loving come together at this point. Put simply, residential communities are where individuals can make mistakes in human relationships, learn from them and move on. All this is part of the formation of wisdom, and the integration of spirituality, academic learning and pastoral care can take place in a residential community. Here we come to the third point raised above about training. Training is about acquiring core skills; it is, second, about residence; third, it is about the integrated nature of the curriculum.

It is also clear that this integration of academic study, worship and pastoral skills is at the heart of the debate as to whether collaborative ministry and leadership can inform each other. Leadership is shown to be possible as a result of character formation. That formation of personal character is the result of this integration of study, worship and pastoral skills. But equally, collaborative ministry is shown in the working together of staff and students, in the different aspects of college life: study, worship and pastoral practice. In other words, both leadership (character formation) and collaboration are shown to be possible as study; worship and pastoral practice come together, but in different ways. One leads into character formation; the other into collaboration together of staff and students as we work at the training alongside each other. *It is possible to form both leaders and collaborative ministry without there being a conflict between them.*

What leadership and collaboration focus on here in this college needs to be lived out across the wider Church. Here the examples given in this collection of essays from across the globe are important. We need to nurture and build such communities here in Wales as well. The pragmatics of ministry requires that there is interplay between what is going on in parishes and ministerial training. Increasingly as clergy are trained and retrained in the practice of Christian collaborative leadership in dioceses and districts, we shall place students in such parishes.[28] It would require a separate chapter to describe how such leadership might be carried out, and how there can be training for it.[29]

However, the overall point is clear. Character formation and the community (or collaborative) discernment of wisdom: these are the components of ordination training at the start of the twenty-first century in Wales. We are in a very different place from a century ago, but we see no salvation in simply relying on the development of management skills either. Instead in the complex pattern of forming individuals alongside each other, in an educational community, and sending them to local and geographical communities to exercise a ministry of leadership and collaboration, we see the future of the Church's ministry.

Discerning this wisdom is hard in a culture which now 'corrodes character', and it is no surprise that this process of discernment seems pointless to many. Nevertheless, it is in this process, in this pattern, that local theologies will need to be fashioned. Out of this will come the clergy and laity of the next century. Past generations of students would be surprised, even shocked, at how fluid this pattern may appear, but for us there is no other way to find the discernment of Christ.

In both residential and non-residential training we seek a contextual, collaborative theology. We also are clear that we seek to form leaders in the full stature of Christ (Eph. 4.13). This theology is there to form character and wisdom so that communities can be regenerated in ways that allow human flourishing. This article has sought to show how there is no tension at the end of the day between the formation of character and leadership on the one hand, and collaboration and Local Ministry on the other. In each of these ways, and in both of them together, we seek to follow Christ. It is a worthy vision for the next century, developing the wisdom of the past and taking it forward in new ways.

Notes

1 C. Brown, *The Death of Christian Britain*, London: Routledge, 2000.
2 Bob Jackson, *Hope for the Church*, London: Church House Publishing, 2002.
3 Archbishops' Council's Working Party Report, *Mission-Shaped Church*, London: Church House Publishing, 2004.
4 Bob Jackson, unpublished paper for the diocese of Monmouth, 2003 (available from the authors).
5 David Faulkner, *Crime, State and Citizen*, Winchester: Waterside Press, 2001, p. 82.
6 Faulkner, *Crime, State and Citizen*, p. 28.
7 Robin Greenwood, *Transforming Priesthood*, London: SPCK, 1994.
8 Hugh Lavery, *Sacraments*, London: Darton, Longman & Todd, 1982, p. 24.
9 Richard McBrien, *Catholicism*, New York: HarperCollins, 1994.
10 John Henry Newman, *University Sermons*, London: SPCK, p. 64.
11 John Henry Newman, *Parochial and Plain Sermons*, San Francisco: Ignatius Press, 1987, p. 259.

12 Roger Crisp and Michael Slote (eds) *Virtue Ethics* (Oxford Readings in Philosophy), Oxford: OUP, 1997; Roger Crisp (ed.) *How Should One Live? Essays on the Virtues*, Oxford: OUP, 2000; Peter Berkowitz, *Virtue and the Making of Modern Liberalism*, Princeton: Princeton University Press, 2000; Roger Kotva, *The Christian Case for Virtue Ethics*, Washington, DC: Georgetown University Press, 1997; Gilbert Meilaender, *The Theory and Practice of Virtue*, Notre Dame, IN: University of Notre Dame Press, 1985; Haydon Ramsey, *Beyond Virtue*, London: Palgrave, 2002; Kieran Flanagan and Peter Jupp, *Virtue Ethics and Sociology: Issues of Modernity and Religion*, London: Palgrave, 2000.

13 Duncan Forrester, *The True Church and Morality. Reflections on Ecclesiology and Ethics*, Risk/World Council of Churches: Geneva, 1997, pp. 77–8.

14 Jean Porter, 'Virtue ethics' in Robin Gill (ed.), *The Cambridge Companion to Christian Ethics*, Cambridge: Cambridge University Press, 2001; Stanley Hauerwas, *The Peaceable Kingdom*, London: SCM Press, 1983.

15 Dan Hardy, 'Theological education in the mission of the Church' in D. Hardy (ed.), *Finding the Church: Explorations in Anglican Ecclesiology*, London: SCM Press, 2001.

16 Hardy, 'Theological education', pp. 175–6.

17 Forrester, *The True Church and Morality*, pp. 79–80.

18 Polly Curtis, 'Postcode lottery for university entrants', *Guardian*, Thursday 20 January 2005.

19 Paul Ballard, 'Poverty and change: the churches' response in South Wales 1966–2000', *Expository Times*, 116(2), November 2004. The July–September 2004 edition of *Crucible* is entitled 'On the faultlines of the global city' and has several articles on the contrast of wealth and poverty in London today.

20 Richard Sennett, *The Corrosion of Character: Personal Consequences of Work in the New Capitalism*, London: Norton, 1998; R. Sennett, *Respect: The Formation of Character in an Age of Inequality*, London: Penguin Books, 2004.

21 Forrester, *The True Church and Morality*, pp. 79–80; Hardy, 'Theological education', p. 177.

22 This section owes much to conversations with Revd Dr Graeme Smith, Dean of Non-Residential Training at St Michael's College, Llandaff, and a former senior lecturer at Oxford Brookes University, who is responsible for developing the curriculum at St Michael's College.

23 R. Schreiter, *Constructing Local Theologies*, London: SCM Press, 1985.

24 D. Bonhoeffer, *Life Together*, London: Fortress Press, 1996; D. Bonhoeffer, *The Cost of Discipleship*, London: SCM Press, 1959. There is an excellent discussion of this point by Haddon Willmer, 'Costly discipleship' in John de Gruchy (ed.), *The Cambridge Companion to Dietrich Bonhoeffer*, Cambridge: Cambridge University Press, 1999.

25 Willmer, 'Costly discipleship', pp. 182–3.

26 Ministry Division of the Church of England Hind Task Groups Draft Reports for Consultation, 'The learning environment of the trainee minister', December 2004, p. 26.

27 Ministry Division, 'The learning environment', p. 26.

28 St Michael's College is an active participant in the Llandaff leadership-training programme for parishes run by the CME officer, Revd Adrian Berry.

29 John Adair and John Nelson (eds), *Creative Church Leadership*, London: Canterbury Press, 2004.

11

Leadership

PHIL KIRK

The world is not perishing for new leadership models. It is perishing for want of a Church that can *be* the good news of Jesus to the poor. If leadership can play a role in helping the Church to organize for that task, then, and only then, is the question of leadership a worthwhile consideration. With this in mind a few observations are presented here about leadership that are drawn from the experience of working with church leaders practising leadership. The aim is to provoke thinking among those who take seriously the need to build models of leadership that are appropriate for their particular contexts and have the capacity to create, nurture and sustain revitalized churches within their communities.

The Church as the body of people providing the Christian witness is always changing. How it manages change matters if it is to be effective and relevant in providing that witness. There are different popular portrayals of these changes in the Anglican Church in the UK today. One is of a Church in lack: fewer clergy, smaller congregations and diminishing resources. The perception is of a group of people trapped in their own institutions, caught up in their own affairs, fevered in their disputes, largely ignoring the rest of the world, and in turn being ignored by it. Another picture is that of churches engaging with their communities in different local projects, joining forces with other local churches from different denominations, working across clergy and laity divides. This second image is of a Church invigorated and with new purpose and relevance. Both pictures present their own challenge.

In the first picture of decline, the challenge to leadership is to face up to realities, and seek creative responses that are more imaginative and hopeful than simply managing decline, or trying to preserve institutional forms and practices. In the second and more relational picture of the church integrated in its community, the challenge to leadership is to find forms of leadership that are more suited and appropriate than the older hierarchical ones.

Providing good church leadership is a continuing work, fashioned through God's grace and human effort. The primary task for leadership is to meet the needs of the time and the place in which all are called to be the Church of Christ. The ideas presented here come from the experience of working with church leaders who have been, and are, grappling with what good leadership in the Church means, and how it can be provided. In their different ways these church leaders were agreed in seeing leadership as essentially regenerative, its aim to revive and renew a spirit or a movement that serves God's mission in their changing local neighbourhoods and communities.

The thoughts in this chapter have been developed out of work over four years with church leaders who have been engaged in providing leadership in parishes and benefices where Collaborative or Mutual Ministry has been the goal. The principal method used was to invite participants to meet as a group once every two months over the period of a year. The groups, typically eight to ten people in each, brought to the sessions stories of 'live' incidents which in some way presented them with a leadership dilemma. Each person told his or her story and then the group critically reflected on it through a structured process. Those listening to the story were invited to notice and share what the story triggered for them. These interpretations of what was going on in the story provided a window into the assumptions and theories about leadership held by the interpreters themselves. In this way the stories and the discussions they generated provided a vehicle for surfacing the theories about leadership held by members of the group. Once surfaced the group was able to critique the theories-in-use, comparing and contrasting the different perspectives, and as a result develop insights and make decisions about the thinking and practice of leadership in the different benefices and local ministry groups.

Mental models

An early discovery was the impact on relations between people when competing models of leadership were at play among different members in team ministry groups. The more the group was able to bring to awareness and talk about how these mental models converged or diverged and the impact they were having on their work, the better was that group able to work together. One example where this did not work was a 'team ministry group' whose shared aim was 'to develop ways of ministering that allowed all members of the church to use their gifts for the glory of God'. In the working out of how this was to be achieved, different thinking was revealed. One group member, the rector, spoke of the need to establish authority relations where some individuals could be 'reined in', and control could be exercised. Another member of the same group held the view of collaboration as participation between people who were in positions of 'total equality'. This person said, 'I never know how to cope with someone who does not want to be a team player, and needs to be in control.' The reality was that there was a way of coping. That was to keep quiet about these divergent perspectives about team leadership at team meetings, and to have conversations 'off line' with, among others, the individual's spiritual director. It is the capacity of a group to talk together, to create and pursue its visions, and work through the 101 obstacles, controversies and conflicts that beset its work that marks out partnership leadership. In espousing unity in the wider body of the Church, there is a quiet witness in the leadership's own workings.

Casting leadership heroes

One 'deep-wired' model of leadership is that of the heroic leader, which survives despite all the rhetoric about collaborative leadership.[1] In this model to think about leadership is to think about the chief executive of a company, the vicar of a parish, and so on. Such a 'top of the house' perspective of leadership goes beyond institutional role and status and enters the domain of myths and heroes. It pervades thinking not just because it is embedded in the sociology of bureaucracy and experience of organizational hierarchy. Culture and the politics of power and control are also at play. The popular cultural heroes of comics, films and television are leaders with extraordinary ability who take care of those less able. These repeating narratives create archetypal heroes, who protect their communities, and lead them out of danger. This, coupled with calls in public life today for leaders who can turn round the fortunes of ailing companies, or modernize public services, makes leadership a heavy word.

Weighed down by so many descriptors – 'decisive', 'servant', 'transformational', 'charismatic' – leadership has reached gigantic proportions. So much so that it is no wonder that in our imaginations it is only giants who are capable of exercising leadership. We can pretend to be giants, or that some among us are so. But it is all illusion. Giants are mythical and leadership as an activity for giants is a prevailing and continuing myth. Myths and illusions do, however, have a real effect. The projected power given to a few 'leaders' by the many 'non-leaders' creates a configuration of power patterning among a community of people that can be taken as the norm, when in fact it is simply a social construction. Leadership in such a construction becomes established as a function of the few.

It may be imagined that such a narrowly distributed conception of organizational leadership is a calculated trick of the minority to exercise control over the majority. In many ways it is the reverse. Anxiety is present in all social interaction when people come together to engage in a task of some description. How will we get on together? How will conflicts emerge and can they be managed without the group disintegrating? Will I fit in, or will I be rejected from the group? The anxieties provoked by such questions cause people to look to a leader who can deal with such worries. This propensity of groups to get diverted from the task which brought them together in the first place, and spend their energies devising ways of avoiding anxiety, was identified by Wilfred Bion (1961). He found that groups would work hard to find an all-powerful leader. The assumption the group makes (unconsciously) is that it must depend on a leader to deliver it from its anxieties. This, in Bion's term, is the 'basic assumption' of dependency. It is an alternative to the group exercising leadership itself in engaging with its task.

Be it through guile, charm, seduction, a leader who the group thinks will save it is put in place. He or she is showered with accolades and then, when at some point proving to be only mortal and unable to fulfil the extraordinary expectations of the group, is ingloriously rejected. The search for a new saving leader commences. If the fault is located with the leader, the validity of the basic assumption, that it is only a leader that can sort out the group's problems, remains unchallenged. The cycle of all praise and all blame to the leader thus continues. Much of this is done unconsciously and is seen in the psychoanalytical perspective as a social defence against anxiety. The conferment of the leadership function on the heroic leader can lead to dependency and possibly indolence in the rest. The refuge provided by the title 'followers' allows responsibility for leadership to be ascribed away from themselves.

Perhaps dependency is paralleled in church leadership. Could resistance to the idea of leadership as a wider communal responsibility (the priesthood of all believers) be as much to do with dependency as it is to do with theology or ecclesiology? Could it be that a basic dependency in the Church is that we must have a priest in our midst to be priest for all? Thus ordered, a priest as 'shepherd' is to get on with 'church business', and the congregation as a 'flock' contents itself with the business of congregating. The Diocese of Bath and Wells in its programme of 'changing lives' quotes Hans Ruedi Weber in its message to the diocese: 'Laity are not the helpers of the clergy so that the clergy can do their job . . . but the clergy are the helpers of the whole people of God, so that the laity can be the church.'

When leadership of a system is a product of dependency, the system as a whole is diminished. The capacity of a community to shape its future, to organize its endeavour and to change itself in the doing, is reduced. If, however, leadership can be viewed as the goal of the system as a whole and the work of all in it, we begin to nurture, develop, build and sustain leadership capacity in the system as a whole. Terms variously used to connote the essence of this collective view of leadership are 'partnership leadership', or 'distributed leadership', or 'community leadership', or 'system leadership', or 'collaborative leadership', or 'inclusive leadership'. How can such forms of leadership be developed?

Collective leadership

The concept of organizational role analysis (Reed, 2000) gives us a way into a more collective approach to leadership. For individuals to play their part in a collective enterprise, they need to have in their minds an idea of their role within the system of which they are a part. The origin of the term 'role' was a rolled parchment from which actors in classical Greek theatre read their scripted lines. Yet there is another way of looking at role, something much less fixed and prescribed. In Reed's words, 'to take a role implies being able to formulate or discover, however intuitively, a regulating principle inside one, as a person, to manage what one does in relation to the requirements of the situation one is in'. The fashioning of one's role involves the person identifying the aim of the system he or she belongs to, taking ownership of that aim as a member of the system, and choosing the action and personal behaviour which from their position best contribute to achieving the aim (Reed, 2000:2). In this way we establish our purpose, identity and validity in the enterprise. We are able to prioritize what matters. To take up one's role in this way is an individual act of leadership. The more all members of an enterprise take up their respective roles in relation to one another for the achievement of a common enterprise, the more we see collective leadership. Does such collective leadership imply the demise of organizational-wide leadership roles, the chief executive, or the bishop in the diocese or the priest in the parish?

The warp and weft of leadership

The roles of people who have boundary-spanning responsibilities are crucial. They have a vital role in setting a framework within which enterprise can flourish. If organizational leadership is located entirely with these 'top of the house' individuals we have a monochromatic view of institutional leadership. A more integrated view of leadership sees leadership capacity residing in every one of the people who are members of the institution and who have a part to play in the enterprise. Leadership thus becomes a relational process of organizational members, irrespective of position or status, taking up their role as they together contribute to the purposes of the enterprise. This, of course, would include those with wider spans of responsibility than others. A metaphor that illustrates this is weaving. System leadership of the kind described here incorporates both the art and the labour that one sees in weaving. There is a warp and a weft to it. The warp represents those people who have senior organizational roles – boundary-spanning roles. From their system-wide perspectives, they are able to provide the warp – the vertical strands. The creative patterning of the weft around the warp represents the contributions of the host of other members working on their own or in clusters. Without the weft, leadership becomes 'warped' – a one-sided affair. Without the warp, there is no holding framework for the weft to find creative expression.

How is it possible to build such leadership capacity in a system of people engaged in collective purposeful action within particular environments? It is the toil in the mill that produces the fine cloth in the shop. So too the development of system leadership requires the labour of people and the grace of God.

Building leadership capacity

The word 'capacity' in the context of development denotes 'a containing space whose nature enables something to happen. Capacity is a potential that is only realized in use. A capacity develops through action or shrinks through neglect' (French, 1999:1218). The inquiry process invites people in an enterprise to critically review their leadership and plan to develop or enhance it. It involves reviewing the extent to which they are connected to a shared vision (*seeing together*), the extent to which they are realizing their visions (*walking together*), and the extent the members are able to engage in constructive dialogue with each other (*talking together*). The stronger they are in each, the stronger is their collective leadership. Attending to this work of building leadership capacity is not neat and can never be complete. It is always work in progress. The three dimensions are interconnected, each affected by and affecting the other two.

Connective leadership: learning to see together

The aim of leadership is to mobilize collective human effort in pursuit of worthy enterprise. The enterprise must have a binding capacity. In a church, essentially a voluntary association, there must be a spirit about the place – an ethos; an image of what and who the church is – a mission; and an inspiring view as to where it is heading, what it is seeking to achieve – a vision. These are the things that hold people together, connected in an enterprise they value. The leadership work of establishing this connectivity is the process, which I call learning to see together. People become connected in an enterprise as they learn how to see together. This involves giving the various people and groups that make up the church the opportunity to voice their aspirations and, through their different voices, see if there is a commonality of purpose that is sufficient to bind them in collective enterprise. It is a process that connects people to their inner desires and dreams. It also connects people, different groups, who despite or perhaps because of their difference see the value of journeying together in a project they all value. In this way a community of interest, a community of action, a community of practice, is established and sustained. It is not a once-and-for-all activity. Connective leadership is an ongoing process that needs continuing attention as needs and circumstances of the community change.

In any serious attempt to attain connection, disconnection is always a prospect; once the vision is clear, some may not find it possible to join. Managing disconnection is a real act of leadership. It must also be a loving act of leadership, to release people to find connection elsewhere. Where, for example, the purpose is to create a church where lay and clergy work together in creative and mutually enabling partnership, some people may find they are unable to sign up to such a task. Connective leadership is hard-edged. It is not sentimental. Having naïve rose-coloured assumptions about unity is as bad as perceiving divergence as deviance or – worse – as an act of betrayal. Its aim is the pursuit of a good-enough unity. Its task is to work at seeing how unity may find its best possible expression among people in the circumstances and contexts in which they find themselves.

Collective empowerment: learning to walk together

This is about communal action. It happens best when members of a group feel they are in partnership with others and doing something of value. Within this there is a very human need to feel valued for oneself and for one's contribution. Collective empowerment is about individuals or different groupings or stakeholders knowing their part in the partnership, and being valued for it. It is also about individuals relating to each other in concerted, collaborative and purposeful action to make good things happen. This can be expressed as learning to walk together. As people work out this relational dynamic of working together, they are being empowered for action and being empowered through action. The term 'walking' is used because it connotes journey, movement, where scenes change. Establishing individual as well as collective identity, role and purpose are outcomes of collective empowerment.

The need for members of the enterprise to work out their roles in relation to one another is fundamental to collective empowerment. Role is a governing idea. It governs how we play our part in a collective enterprise. The process of organizational role analysis as developed by the Tavistock Institute (Reed, 1976) involves role-finding, role-making and role-taking. Role-*finding* is about establishing clarity of purpose, knowing our primary purpose in the system of which we are a part. To do this we need to identify the system we are in and identify with its aim. Not to do this would be working for our own ends within a system that we simply use for our own purposes.

Once we have clarified the purpose of our role, we need to be able to discern how we are to pursue that purpose. This is about role-*making*, and it has an internal and an external dimension. Both are about accessing power to achieve the purposes of our role. The internal dimension is concerned with drawing on who we are as individuals, our personality, experiences, skills and competencies, our values, motivations, our knowledge about ourselves, our worst and best selves. Through this inner gaze we are able to draw on the uniqueness of our individuality. Never has there been another person like us in this position. In all humility we become aware of the possibilities that we can achieve in our role, because of just who we are as people fearfully and wonderfully made by God. Finding our worth allows us to be centred in our role. The external dimension to role-finding is about being street-wise in the system we are in. By getting to know the highways, byways and dead-ends we develop organizational satellite navigation, which is as much a political aid as a navigational one! We get to know who will help and who will not. We learn how to forge strategic alliances with people inside and outside the system to make things happen.

If role-making provides us with the wherewithal to do our work, role-*taking* is about doing it. It is about seeing opportunities opening up and seizing the moment, taking action in the unfolding, changing drama of organizational life. It is about carrying out our prescribed tasks, but it is also about how we exercise the myriad choices that we have to make about how we will initiate or respond to events.

When we take up our role with clarity, authority and confidence, we inhabit our role. Taking up one's role individually is a leadership act. When several people take up their roles in relation to one another we build and exercise collective leadership. The experience of being part of a collective action where people create and accomplish amazing things together is one never to forget. Witnessing this in others is also a transforming experience. One example is the Truth and Reconciliation Commission, which provided a unique act of nation-building in South Africa. Collective empowerment, the act of walking together, is about communion and agency. It is about relating and acting, where 'power with' rather than 'power over' is the determining factor. Collective empowerment, it must be said, comes with a warning! It will disturb, and can be experienced as disturbing. For example, the priest, the lay member, the diocesan officer, may find they need to work out new roles and new ways of relating to one another from their differing roles.

Dialogue: learning to talk together

The ability to see together and to walk together depends on how well we are able to talk together. The way we talk together, and the stories and myths we generate, creates its own reality. The realities we create through dialogue, within ourselves and with others, shape our thinking and action. We construct our realities together. So if organizations are social constructions, and we primarily construct them through language, then it is through language that we sustain or change them. New people come into a team, or a parish, or a diocese, and have their perspective of what is going on, and what to them seems to have been going on in the past. These new pictures have the potential to create an alternative picture in people's minds of who and how they are. This is especially so if the new people are powerful either through personality or position, say a new priest, or a new bishop.

Power relations pattern the conversations of people in any group (or wider system). For instance, in team meetings, by seeing who speaks, who chooses what to speak or not speak about, whose voices carry weight and whose voices remain silent, unheard or ignored, we get a feel of the way power moves and works in the group. By becoming more aware of the power patterns, it becomes possible to alter them. The 'open' discussions we have at meetings ('let's throw it open to the meeting') are never 'open'. They proceed to follow the default patterns that have been established over time. These conversations are 'safer', more predictable, but usually keep hidden the things people want to say, and formulaic conversations continue, sometimes leaving things unsaid, with people leaving frustrated and angry with others and themselves. This continues until the next meeting when the same things are said, and the same things left unsaid. Eventually the frustrations and anger go and people either leave or stay having given up the desire to speak their truths, or forget the alternative picture they once had and wanted to share. Dialogue in its true sense, the flow of meaning between people, is not easy.

Dialogue is a process for creating meaning, identity and purpose. It is a process whereby a group engages with its realities, and constructs pathways for action. Central to the process is respecting the parties involved in the dialogue. Dialogue encourages all voices to be heard, including the 'dissenting' voice (see Arbucke, 1993:1). In this way the group can work with its differences and not view them negatively or fearfully. It can explore alternatives in order to affirm what it wants to keep or to change. This kind of dialogue looks for the assumptions at play that lie behind the contributions people make. It seeks to surface those assumptions and examine them. This practice of reflexivity (reflecting in action) enables us, in the midst of our talking, to notice the emotions being generated, the anger, the resistance, the apathy, and to work at finding out about what is going on and dealing with it. This is hard talk: it is hard to do, and is not timorous. It demands that we engage one another in respectful ways, and not in a whiff of 'niceness' that conceals resentments. If we can learn to talk to each other in these ways, we have robust conversations, not enfeebled ones. Such conversations allow us to live in the question, and present opportunity for creating answers and constructing action.

To establish dialogue there needs to be a container. The way the person who chairs the meeting, or leads, does matter. By being clear about the principles that govern discussion, they hold the anxieties present when people are real with one another. Principles that help to establish dialogue include slowing down the conversations, respecting what is said and those who are saying it, by suspending our 'noble certainties' and trying to understand the other's perspective, not just being the advocates of our own. Dialogue challenges us to surface and confront the assumptions operating in the group. New forms of inter-organizational working with stakeholders from different backgrounds find that the usual patterns of doing things in their own set-ups work less well in joint operations. In such situations people need to work out a new way of being together for the reality that marks their association. Learning to talk together is not the same as being taught to talk according to the custom of one of the partners. Talk can change customs: that is its potential, and that is the point.

For people in ministry groups the invitation is to attend to the conversations they have. In this is the challenge to notice *how* they talk together, not just to notice *what* they talk about. Developing such attention and care will build the group's capacity to have powerful conversations that create vision, mobilize energy and inspire action.

To conclude, the observations in this chapter are offered as a contribution to the thinking of those engaged or wishing to engage with the task of developing a new communal approach to leadership in the Church. Such leadership will be concerned with drawing people together in creative, life-enhancing and transforming ways. In doing so it will give graceful witness of a Church that helps people to encounter God and the love God has for all people.

References

Arbucke, G., *Refounding the Church: Dissent for Leadership*, London: Geoffrey Chapman, 1993.

Bion, W., *Experiences in Groups*, London: Tavistock Publications, 1961.

French, R., 'The importance of capacities in psychoanalysis and the language of human development', *The International Journal of Psychoanalysis*, 80(6), December 1999.

Reed, B., 'Organisational role analysis: a training method based on the Tavistock/Grubb approach to learning about behaviour', in C. Cooper (ed.), *Developing Social Skills in Managers: Advances in Group Training*, London: Association of Teachers in Management, 1976.

Reed, B., *An Exploration of Role as Used in the Grubb Institute*, London: The Grubb Institute, 2000.

Afterword: Evaluating Local Ministry for the future of the Church

DANIEL W. HARDY

Introduction

The passionate concern expressed in this book is for a Church truly responsive to God's mission in the world, with a vitality commensurate with this mission. It finds one set of important clues to such a Church in what is variously called 'local', 'total', 'mutual', 'shared', 'total life caring', or 'collaborative' ministry and mission, which have released so much hope and energy for those churches which have taken them up in various parts of the world.

I can recall when I was moderator of what was then the General Ministerial Examination of the Church of England 25 years or so ago, how difficult it was to assess the value of this 'new form of ministry'. That was partly because it was then (and often still is) much less a new kind of way of 'being Church' than a way of providing priests locally where none were otherwise available. It was also because, by the educational standards then (and largely still) used, 'Ordained Local Ministry' seemed less than it should be; given prevailing notions of ministry, it was difficult to condone an ordained ministry in which the persons involved could serve only in the congregation which originally called them. If, however, this was in fact a new way of being Church, the standards we were using those many years ago were too limited for a proper assessment.

It is still too difficult to take stock of what has been going on, either to know what has been happening or to have an appropriate way of appraising it. Simply to have the reports and analyses of 'Local Ministry' – we will use that as a generic name – in this book helps us begin to understand and weigh up an important way of being Church which has been underway for many years now in scattered places. At the same time, it is important to recognize that Local Ministry is still evolving in practice, and any portrayal or appraisal is at least somewhat tentative.

Evaluating Local Ministry raises the large question which we must address in this chapter: *how to appreciate and appraise this way of being Church, both theologically and ecclesiologically, and how to identify ways of developing it for the future.* There are three main reasons why this is an important undertaking:

1 Unless it is helped to be self-critical, Local Ministry may easily become a set of instinctively formed and self-justifying practices adopted in certain circumstances, and it will continue to be seen by others as a purely pragmatic and experimental move, a kind of 'try it and see' sort of church, uncertainly related to traditional ways.
2 Unless its value theologically and ecclesiologically is shown, we will not be able to identify how it may be significant for the life of the whole Church within the purposes of God for all social life and institutions.
3 Until its limitations become apparent, we will not know how it needs development.

Local Ministry among different ways to be Church

The question of the position of Local Ministry among different ways of being Church is still unresolved. In an order moving from negative to positive, is it

1 *an aberration* from traditional ways?
2 *one among a number* of ways?
3 a form to be *preferred under certain circumstances*?
4 a form *always to be preferred for local churches*?

As we have seen in this book, the proponents of Local Ministry mainly take the second or third views, while resisting the first (and those – diocesan bishops, for example – who follow it in practice, obstructing the development of Local Ministry). While many of them also cite Roland Allen as a precursor, he certainly took the fourth view, and they rarely make such a strong claim as he did, that it should be normal for local churches to be established and left to develop in the power of the Holy Spirit without further intervention. At this point, apart from denying the first option as a premature judgement, it is impossible to judge between these alternatives.

There is one further option which ought also to be considered seriously, that Local Ministry is a way of raising up characteristics that ought always to appear in the Church, and which are therefore important as a 'general formula'[1] for ordering church life. It may be one way – though possibly not the only one – of identifying some of the *primary patterns* that need to be used wherever the Church is, while the particular ways in which they are followed might be – to use an old designation – 'indifferent',[2] suitable to particular circumstances but not universally applicable. We need to keep watch for evidence that Local Ministry identifies what ought to be primary patterns for church life.

How to understand the Church: the question of criteria

Even to approach the question of how to appraise Local Ministry as a way of being Church, however, requires that we find how to understand the Church. That is a particularly difficult preliminary assignment.

A noticeably popular way to describe the Church is to use 'slogans' or 'words' which identify important characteristics of life together in the Church, which people can recognize and build on, like 'community', 'imagination', 'the interweaving of practices with the truth of God', the 'energy' or 'godly power' of the Holy Spirit that 'sets people free to discover the kingdom of God', and the 'blessing' that comes from them.[3] Using words and slogans in this way is engaging and evocative, and it attracts, holds together and liberates people with differing expectations and gifts. (This particular set of words was used to describe a church best viewed as a 'hybrid', where a highly educated part-time priest has fostered a church order incorporating many characteristic features of Local Ministry.)

There is more resistance to identifying clear criteria and applying them to the Church. Analysing well-known patterns of church life, in order to go 'upstream' (by raising expectations) or to go 'downstream' (by reducing expectations), unlocks anxious questions about how to be Church today. There may be general agreement about the need for new ways of enabling the Church to coincide with God's purposes, and for new ways by which it can further these purposes for and in the world. As to finding how to make headway with these, there is much less agreement; and churches – whether parishes or dioceses – jealously guard their right to decide!

Lacking some stronger criteria, however, dangers confront the Church: long-established ways of being the Church are simply perpetuated in unexamined and ineffective versions, and new ones are invented ad hoc. In response to the apparent decline in churches which follow old ways, the question is now, 'Why *not* experiment with new ways of being Church?' Perhaps the 'emergent Church' is the future.

> the emerging church of the 21st century may have more in common with the church of the apostolic era, than with the church of the 20th century.
>
> many ancient practices of faith and ways of being communal are being re:booted and morphed for the needs of the future church. as Leonard Sweet writes, 'our faith is ancient. our faith is future. we're old-fashioned. we're new-fangled. we're orthodox. we're innovators. we're postmodern christians.'[4]

The result is a marketplace of different 'styles of being Church', each of them pursued self-justifyingly – as 'what works here' – and each prey to circumstantial pressures. Local Ministry is no less affected by these problems than any other form of social life in the Church.

The reasons for such a plurality of expectations for life are not far to seek. They are traceable to uncertainties about the meaning of Christian faith for today, differences of context and circumstances, and the freedom and autonomy of individuals and groups:

1 Different social circumstances have forced church life to adapt itself to different contexts, raising the question of whether there *can be* a common set of standards for church life.
2 Puzzlement about how to relate to social life that has become predominantly secular, and how to reach or include those who follow these standards, tends to diminish the value placed on distinctively Christian criteria.
3 Changing social circumstances have brought genuine dilemmas about the forms of social order best suited to the future of human society.[5] Like public democratic institutions in the West, it has been difficult to adapt existing forms of ecclesial social order to different contexts and normative claims, and to mediate between the

disagreements which these differences have generated. The sense of a common purpose for society has diminished, and there is inner disharmony and division, often over single issues. It is unclear how different forms of church life can co-exist.

4 Especially in voluntary institutions, it is easy for individuals (or, for that matter, special interest groups) to opt for social units in which they can have their way,[6] or to oppose forms of order which constrain or challenge their voice and the expression of their interests.[7] Hence, institutions are often kept weak enough to 'hold' people (or special interest groups) by allowing maximum room for their interests.[8]

Like the key words, slogans or evocative descriptions of church life we discussed earlier, these factors acknowledge or encourage diversity, pragmatic experimentation and fluidity of social forms, including a variety of kinds of ministry and mission, both 'traditional' and new, including 'Local Ministry'.

Finding theological and ecclesiological standards

Despite the potential problems in finding criteria for church life, there are several discernibly different levels of criteria by which we can measure it: purely social, generically Christian and definitely theological–ecclesiological.

Level 1: Purely social criteria

In any society, we never have the privilege of starting entirely afresh. We always start 'in the middle', with institutions, people and practices already formed in particular ways, often supported by strongly held rationales. In any social institution of which we are part, therefore, we tacitly concur with:

1 how it *is*, its 'being' or 'state';
2 the ways by which it is *ordered* in its public life;
3 the ways in which it *acts* day to day;
4 how its people *are with* each other;
5 their *responsibilities* and how they recognize and perform them;
6 *how these tasks are distributed* among them and *co-ordinated*;
7 how all these things *interact with others* in wider circles;
8 how this body *relates* to the wider society of which it is part.

All these are operative in practice as we live in a society. They are so manifold, so interwoven and so much embedded in what we are and do that it is difficult to think what they are and shape them. The temptation is to simplify them to one particular aspect or task, or a few of them.

Level 2: Generically Christian criteria

The characteristics reviewed so far are those of any social institution. How they operate in the Church is a more difficult matter, and involves such questions as these:

1 Are its being and social structure traceable to the being and law of God?
2 Is it a coherent pattern of social actions which shows God's action in and for the world (what is often called *missio dei*)?
3 Is it transformative for the social deficiencies of those involved?
4 Does it interact with, and seek the transformation of, other social life?
5 Does it evoke awareness of, and directedness to, the kingdom of God?

These questions test how far the church as an ordinary social institution is established theologically and ecclesiologically, how far it is *Church*. And such criteria, one supposes, can be met by churches generically.

Level 3: Specific theological and ecclesiological criteria

For some, the questions just listed arouse worries about whether the way the Church is, acts and directs itself are so directly linked to the being and actions of God in bringing the world to the kingdom of God. There can be no doubt that this is the major intellectual question surrounding all that the Church is and stands for. This is where we find problems in a common view of the Church. It appears that Christian faith and Church have not been well enough commended to attract those not already inclined to them, especially those whose lives are lived by other standards, and who no longer see the point of faith and Church.

All that notwithstanding, let us try to give a defensible account of an Anglican conception of a faithful Church, telling what the Church is in the purposes of God, at least ideally. In such a Church, there is a corporate vision of the infinitely intensive identity of the holy God, of the God

1 whose 'being is law to his working',[9] and who is always active in gathering his people;
2 whose 'nature is always to have mercy', who is consistent in just and compassionate care for those whom he creates and sustains, acting or working constantly in and for them to the point of extending himself – his grace – fully for all people;
3 whose care reaches into the whole of their lives – even into their self-interest – and 'covers' them in their successes and failures by Christ, his life, death and resurrection, thereby redirecting the course of their lives and giving them – by his Spirit – the promise of fulfilment in God's kingdom;
4 whose just and compassionate care in its full extent is actually mapped onto the Church in its mission, where the Church – properly speaking –
   (a) shares fully in the range of human life and activity in its particular situation;
   (b) acts as the full apostolic self-extension of God in the world;
   (c) shows the constant just compassion of God among human beings;
   (d) in their diversity and divisions restores them to unity;
   (e) in their limitations and failures helps them to be holy, nurturing them in likeness to God;
   (f) spreads into the whole world as God's catholic work;
   (g) manifests the inner dynamic of the Spirit of God in the world;
   (h) brings the world to the kingdom of God.

Altogether, this means that as God is, so God acts in Christ, and – by the Holy Spirit – in the Church where the Church acts in its mission to the world in accordance with God's activity.

While it is common enough to judge churches, their ministry and their mission by the first two levels of criteria, it is the third level which uncovers the full distinctiveness of the Church among the plethora of social institutions in the world, and also the nature of its deep involvement with them. And such a view can give the Church the clear sense of its nature – its origins, priorities, order and goal – by which to shape and conduct its life and practice.

This set of criteria allows us to measure the strengths and weaknesses of all forms of ministry and mission. For Local Ministry, it gives indications of its strengths, where it needs to be developed, and its special contribution to theology and ecclesiology.

A Church for the people in mission

One characteristic implicit in all three levels of criteria is how the Church is and acts in ways which are self-involving for its people and are also interactive with the surrounding society. Is it of such a kind as to be immediate to its people and its context, or is it somehow removed from them, to the point where they are more detached? Are they effectively involved in the *missio dei* embodied in the Church, and therefore with God acting with human life in the world to bring its fulfilment, or are they bystanders?

Local Ministry is above all a serious attempt to reinvigorate church life for its people and for particular contexts, to reconstitute, organize and energize a new form of ministry and mission in these conditions. How, and how far, does it succeed, and how does it need to develop? We need first to ask that question by using the three levels of criteria just identified.

If we use Level 1 criteria, it is clear that in Local Ministry there is a significant operational match between a way of being the Church, a form of ministry–mission and actual practice, that is close interaction in what people do between being Church, functions and outcomes. The Church is those who act together in and for God's mission. And underlying this is a passionate conviction that the being of the Church (its form) *becomes* real as it acts effectively (its functions) in and through people toward particular ends (its goal), in what is a generative dynamic.

The same might be claimed for other ways of being Church, however. Where is the difference? In other ways of being the Church, its being (form) and operation is often conceived in more limited ways, with more limited purposes and outcomes: for example, a more perfect church visible in perfection of worship, education, wonderful buildings and thorough pastoral care. (I knew a church in the USA where the rector discouraged members from attracting new people, 'because I cannot care for them'; to use a filling-station image, the church should only have the number for which its rector could supply pastoral care.) This comparison brings to light what might be one of the most interesting aspects of Local Ministry, the coupling of intense co-operative action with an expansive horizon, unrestricted mission to the whole world.

If we move to Level 2 criteria, where the Church is theologically understood, we see how important it is that in Local Ministry the being of the Church is traced to God's action in baptism, by which the whole people of God are ordered for active ministry and mission. That is,

1 The Church is those who are baptized: in accordance with the 1982 Lima Documents, *Baptism, Eucharist and Ministry*,[10] Baptism is seen as forming 'the whole of humanity to become God's people'.
2 And as baptized, all people have gifts – which need to be discovered – which are to be actively used in ministry.

This is a highly significant claim, linking ordinary social standards to theological ones. Having made the claim, however, the conception of ministry at work seems to become more vague, and surely needs further development: how does this ministry show the coherence of God's action in and for the world, interact with and transform human life, and direct people to the kingdom of God? Despite these limitations, Local Ministry provides a strong contrast to conventional understandings of the Church, where the action of God in baptism is not of such primary significance, where baptism is considered only the first step in a sequence of qualifications for ministry: ministry is restricted to those baptized *and* confirmed *and* trained *and* experienced *and* (often) ordained.[11]

If we begin to use Level 3 criteria for Local Ministry, where there are much more specific theological and ecclesiological criteria, there are more questions to be raised than Local Ministry provides answers to. The themes underlying those criteria are how the intensity of who God is, is shown in the consistency of God's just and compassionate actions for the whole world, reaching and restoring every aspect of the world for the kingdom of God, and how this is mapped onto the Church and its mission. Like most conceptions of God, Church and ministry today, Local Ministry needs to give more careful consideration to these issues, to why and how it is what it is and does what it does.

Communal action

Continuing with Level 3 standards, we find the basis for Local Ministry both strong and weak. One of the most important – or most often mentioned – descriptions of Local Ministry is that it generates new awareness of community, and in some accounts this is likened to the inner-trinitarian relations of God. Despite the prominence of this correlation of human community and divine community in theology in the last 20 years, however, it describes a rather inert correspondence between the two: it does not tell us how God is God in always actively gathering and ordering the people of God for the kingdom of God. Nor, typically, does it say much about the way in which God works through and beyond the Church, by consistently just and compassionate action. Here is where we would do well to recall some recent words of the new Pope Benedict XVI, 'One becomes similar to God to the degree that one becomes one who loves.' How do Church and mission, as conceived in Local Ministry, increase people's similarity to God and direct them to the kingdom of God? In a time where it is normal to act primarily for short-term self-interest, this is especially important.

To take another issue, how then do Church and mission, as conceived in Local Ministry, enact the working of God? One of the strengths of Local Ministry is its recognition and nurturing of the gifts of all the people of God. Underlying this is the supposition that people genuinely differ, and that the Church is a diversity of people with distinctive gifts which need to be allowed to flourish in their own right: the Church is a complex gathering of gifted people. Yet it remains a question how these gifts serve and enact the character of the working of God, justice and compassion.

It doesn't help to suggest that these gifts are 'equal'. As gifted, people are equal, but with the diversity of people, their gifts will be expressed in different ways which are not easily comparable. Furthermore, those to whom these gifts are given also differ, and receive what is given differently. In other words, gifts are *particular* and *relational*, both in themselves and for others; it is difficult to compare them, or see them as 'equal'. This is a little like the 'gift' of being parent to children, where the gift differs with each parent and is expressed differently according to the needs of the children.

There is an important reason for this. In God's just and compassionate action, God has made a world where people and things are each and always dependent on God, and reliant on each other in different ways for the meeting of their needs. The world, both in relation to God and in itself, is asymmetrical. 'Gifts' and ministries are not free-standing, but operate relationally as focused on meeting the needs of others; they become ministries when they do meet these differing needs. The 'equality' of gifts and ministries is only in their gracing by God and the intensity with which they are pursued. Since one cannot really compare their efficacy in meeting particular needs, 'equality' does not really apply.

If we look at the characteristics of the Church overall, another issue appears. There will still be standard ministries within which these differentiations occur, those which have to do with basic ways in which people need to be reached, challenged, nurtured and transformed to build them together to the measure of the full stature of Christ and their fulfilment in the kingdom of God:

> The gifts he gave were that some would be apostles, some prophets, some evangelists, some pastors and teachers, to equip the saints for the work of ministry, for building up the body of Christ, until all of us come to the unity of the faith and of the knowledge of the Son of God, to maturity, to the measure of the full stature of Christ.
>
> (Eph. 4.11–13, NRSV)

Somehow, therefore, the differentiation of gifts and ministries, and of their meaning for those who benefit by them, should build unity in Christ and full relation to God. How does this happen?

Ministry and mission together: predefined or actively achieved?

If by necessity people, both in their gifts and in their needs, are as diverse as we have suggested, how can there be a ministry and mission through which unity in Christ and God's kingdom will be built? This is one form of a fundamental question for all creation: how in the diversity and differentiation of the world (its *extensity*, both as created and as fallen through the turning-in on themselves of human beings)[12] are the *intensity* of God's life and purposes to be pursued?

The same question faces the Church: if the intense identity of God (God's being) is known consistently in the diversity and differentiation of creation through God's working there for justice and compassion, for the coming of God's kingdom of peace and love, how does this happen in and through the Church?

During much of the history of the Church, it has seemed that the Church is simply universal by definition, and that its organization and practices should always be the same. The shock came when there was disagreement about its purity, order and practices, at the Reformation for example, when nation-states were first emerging. This modified conceptions of 'universality': thereafter particular regional or national or even worldwide churches defined their universality for themselves and implemented it by ordering their social structure accordingly. This pluriformity has steadily increased through cultural differentiations, and – as we saw earlier – there is much more questioning about whether an agreed theological grounding for the Church is possible, and can now be sustained in its order and practice. The being of the Church is not so much predefined as found continuously, through consistent participation in the *missio dei*.

The implication is highly significant. There are now two standard notions offered in and for the Church, it seems: being Church by *definition* and by *action*:

1 The unity of God in Christ defines what the Church is, and defines the unity of the Church in the world despite its apparent diversity. Hence the Church is predefined as one for the whole world, with the implication:
   (a) that its life and ministry are always fundamentally the same, even if differing by place and time;
   (b) that its ministry is singular, exemplified in a coherent hierarchy of 'corporate persons' who incorporate and proclaim the whole Church from the widest sphere to the smallest place, to whom other forms of ministry are subordinate.
2 The unity of God in Christ in the Church is found through the consistency of the action of the Church in its diversity of ministry and mission, with the implication:
   (a) that there are various forms of ministry and mission suitable to differences of gift and to those towards whom they are directed;

(b) that those with these gifts and expressions actively achieve co-inherence in what they are and do, thereby exemplifying the Church.

The difference between these is simple and fundamental. In the first, the *self-same being of God in Christ* predefines all life and ministry in the Church, whose place is to exemplify it. In the second, the *being of God in Christ by the Holy Spirit* – the consistency of God's just and compassionate working – is lived in and through differences of gift and expression, and is found and understood through its outworking in the elemental movement of the world to its fullness in the kingdom of God.

With the prominence now given to diversity and change, the second of these two ways has become highly important. Without fully realizing it, perhaps, Local Ministry may embody this second way of being Church, and – maybe too readily – may identify itself through its contrast with the first.

There are, nonetheless, some ways in which the two kinds coincide, the first providing a clear notion of the being and self-consistency of God, the second a clear view of how this is actively achieved in the changes and differentiations of the world. And these ways need more attention than they have so far received, the kinds of situation in which ministry and mission occur, and the kinds of education and leadership the Church needs.

Situation and community: what kind of place and what kind of ministry?

There is an important background issue which has to be faced whichever of these two notions of Church is used. The being and finding of the Church happen today in a strongly differentiated social life.

Broadly speaking, there are now three types of social life, each correlated with a particular kind of organization:

1 the *proto-social*, where social units are small, people gather through personal interaction, and responsibilities are distributed by personal negotiation;

2 a *more developed society*, where social units are larger and relations between people are more distant, less personal and more complex,

and social organization is determined by the deliberations of representatives; those elected for the task, by consensus or majority, decide policies for common life, and assign responsibilities to people chosen to carry them out;

3 a *highly developed society*, where social units are still larger and relations are more complex, and are governed by leaders whose task is to preside over the society in its internal and external relations, and by public bodies which approve the actions of the leaders, make and execute laws and regulations, and set up administrative bureaucracy to ensure that the laws and regulations are followed.

Churches follow these three types:

1 a small parish with few people is proto-social in its organization, where everything is 'up close and personal', with a minimum of formal deliberation and action, because the same small number of people must perform tasks;

2 a mid-sized parish is organized through a body (in England a parochial church council) in which chosen representatives deliberate and decide – or delegate such responsibilities to subcommittees – on policies and appoint those (usually unpaid) who are to implement them, relying on the personal appropriateness of those chosen to embody the policies in forms of ministry;

3 a large church, with many members whose relationships are more formal and occasional, will have an elected representative council – often remote from the day-to-day reality of church life – to govern it, which relies heavily on a (usually paid) professional support staff – an administrative bureaucracy – to put policies into effect, with much less personal involvement by members.

Which of these 'seems natural' depends on size and circumstances; not infrequently today, finances determine which type is followed. Whether because an individual church cannot afford the large sum – over \$120,000 in the USA now – needed to pay, house, insure and pension a staff, or because a diocese (as in England) is required to implement a national policy which in effect disallows full-time staff for small (or even mid-sized) churches, the effect is to press churches in the direction of less bureaucratic or representative forms of church life and–or towards the proto-social.

Yet the two ways of being Church – predefined and found through activity – interact:

1 Local Ministry supposes
   (a) that baptism implies for everyone gifts and their use in personal ministry;
   (b) that ministry is radically oriented to the varying task of meeting the needs of others and hence varies with them;
   (c) that church organization is the co-inherence of people in their personal ministries which are 'up close and personal'.
2 The Church as traditionally predefined employs
   (a) the norms, organization and practices of the larger church;
   (b) standardized notions of ministry;
   (c) the emphasis on deliberation, policy and expert practice.

General acceptance of the Church as traditionally predefined, however, makes others suppose that the Church should 'really' follow the procedures of (2); and they are frequently pressed to do this by the bureaucratic requirements of the 'larger church'.

Properly speaking, however, Local Ministry treats the proto-social (a) as normal, not the characteristic features of larger churches (b or c). This has an important consequence: *Local Ministry converts a predefined Church into an active one.* As a personal and active Church, Local Ministry finds the 'being of God in the laws of God's working', by following the consistency of God's just and compassionate working in the active ministry and mission of all the people, moving the world to its fullness in the kingdom of God. It does not deny the need, in some cases, for (b) and (c), but the local church is formed 'from the bottom', not led 'from the top'.

Isn't this a way by which Local Ministry serves as a 'general formula' for what ought always to appear in the Church?

1 Where at first it might appear that Local Ministry happens only in a church in a proto-social situation, gathering and organizing people in personal ways, if the Church is determined by 'following the consistency of God's just and compassionate working in the active ministry and mission of all the people, moving the world to its fullness in the kingdom of God', this will be a formula for all churches, no matter how large, politically organized or bureaucratically administered.

2 When a larger church, knowing that people relate best through direct personal interaction, *encourages* the developing of small units within itself, it is actually acknowledging one aspect of the 'general formula' of Local Ministry. On the other hand, if the larger unit – perhaps for fear of encouraging some kind of aberration – *directs* the formation and operation of small units, it follows the rhetoric of Local Ministry while undermining its insight. That can readily happen when a diocesan policy includes Local Ministry but only where closely controlled or supervised.

3 A further problem emerges with the predominance of oligarchic societies today, where most political power effectively rests with a small segment of society (typically the most powerful). In this case, people are likely to think that the society is really what happens at the level of 'the most powerful'. Accordingly, the practices appropriate to that level will displace – or intrude upon – those appropriate to the smallest and 'least powerful' ones. But if Local Ministry is right, the reverse will be true.

Education, leadership and ordained ministry

In the past, as we have seen, the unity of God in Christ has been taken to define what the Church is, and this includes the suppositions (1) that its life and ministry are always fundamentally the same, and (2) that its ministry is singular, exemplified in a coherent hierarchy of 'corporate persons' who incorporate the whole Church from the widest sphere to the smallest place, who may 'share' their ministry with others. We also saw, however, that diversity and change have brought to the fore another view of the Church. This occurs where an active Church finds the 'being of God in the laws of God's working', by following the consistency of God's just and compassionate working in the active ministry and mission of all the baptized, through which the world is moved to its fullness in the kingdom of God.

Interestingly enough, this 'active' view places a premium on the education, insight and character of those who minister.

1 Especially in a world where people have drifted away from the Church and are unconvinced that it has a valuable contribution to make, the task of communicating the consistency of God's just and compassionate working requires ministry with genuine

wisdom, compassion and sensitivity to the aspirations and needs of others.

2 In the time of the 'predefined Church', however, theological education conferred 'one size fits all' general knowledge, and that sort of knowledge was – and is – nearly always untranslatable into wisdom for the aspirations and needs of people.

3 What is now needed, where the Church is found through active following of God's just and compassionate purpose in the active ministry and mission of all the people, is wisdom to respond to the most fundamental aspirations and needs of people, even where these are presented as coded 'symptoms'.

Significantly, this will call for new conceptions of theological education and formation, not simply forms of the old adapted for wider use.

Given the importance of diversity and differentiation in the activities by which the being of the Church is found through active ministry and mission, the presence of an educated ordained priest seems at first no longer to be necessary. Isn't the main issue to distribute ministries to those who have gifts and exercise them, none with higher standing than any other, and co-inherent in their gifts to meet the needs of the saints? At one level, the clear answer is 'yes'. From that point of view, any church which insists on the special importance of an ordained priesthood might be taken to be a victim of the Anglican 'love affair with clericalism'.

But there are legitimate reasons, both practical and theological, for assigning special importance to an educated ordained priesthood. Some of them are:

1 If the Church is found in the active following of God's just and compassionate working among human beings, this is focused in the sacraments, not only baptism but also the Eucharist; and the Eucharist is presided over by one who actively exemplifies the life and ministry of all those who are entrusted with it in baptism, without displacing it. This is the form of 'corporate personality' appropriate to a Church constituted by active following of God's working.

2 It is abundantly clear that – to put it bluntly – churches want 'leverage' for their building up, from leaders with the education and gifts
    (a) to stimulate and raise them to better ways of being Church; and

(b) to mediate the grace of God by which some act as apostles, some as prophets, some as evangelists, some as pastors and some as teachers.

In other words, these churches want someone *wise in the wisdom of God* to develop them as faithful and to interact with them as they perform other necessary roles. As Richard Hooker once said: 'Without their captains, who will tell them they are faithful?'

3 Where in the calmer communities of the past people had time to assume the responsibilities attendant on the many kinds of lay ministry necessary in a church, today's world conspires against this.

(a) In today's churches, the necessary roles must be done *alongside* other very consuming tasks; and immersion in these tasks is intrinsically valuable to participating in the *missio dei* beyond the Church (as narrowly conceived).

(b) The help of someone capable of co-ordinating the 'extensity' of church life with the 'intensity' of God's purposes and mission is important for their co-inherent ministries. This is not a matter of gifts or willingness, but one of practicality.

4 The roles identified in Ephesians 4 are not simply 'getting the work done', but a series of challenges, and – lest the people involved 'average their talents down to a mean', or subject the personal gifts for each role to the limitations of common or committee understanding – a leader is needed who will help ministers identify and reach their full potential in mission. In other words, leaders are needed who will remind people of, and energize them in, the most fundamental goals which they serve, the flourishing of all people in the kingdom of God, as well as the qualities necessary to serve them.[13] The risk and the promise will draw the utmost from those who are to bring 'the unity of the faith and of the knowledge of the Son of God, maturity in the measure of the full stature of Christ'.

While these are strong reasons for retaining the importance of an educated ordained ministry, the predefined 'template' of church life makes the position of the ordained priest susceptible to misuse; he or she may:

1 *substitute* for the kinds of ministry others should have, attempting to serve in turn as apostle, prophet, evangelist, pastor and teacher, or reserving one such role to him or herself;

2 *dominate* in a proto-social situation, especially where he or she has been sent by the wider Church, like the vicar of a church in the Black Country near Birmingham who thought he had to tell people what to do; without him they would not know what to do;

3 *import* the patterns and preoccupations of more developed social or church situations into situations whose people are primarily concerned with proto-social dilemmas, like the vicar of a small American parish in a modest area who habitually preaches there on the political problems which interest middle-class 'social leaders'.

For these reasons, the position of ordained ministry also needs to be reconsidered to make it appropriate to the notion of Church which underlies Local Ministry.

There are important lessons for both Local Ministry and other ways of being Church in the issues we have discussed, which cannot be ignored. Among them all, the task of actively finding the being of the Church through ministry and mission which follows the just and compassionate working of God in the *missio dei* is the primary issue for all church life today.

Notes

1 In some quarters, this is called a 'heuristic' or an 'algorithm'.

2 While maintaining the great importance of social order in the purposes of God, the classic Anglican theologian Richard Hooker (1554–1600) argued that the ways of organizing the Church were one of the 'things indifferent' to God.

3 Final sermon by Revd Dr Sam Wells to St Mark's Church, Newnham, Cambridge, 10 July 2005.

4 'emerging::church/postmodern::world', <www.emergingchurch.org>, last accessed 2 August 2005.

5 This is parallel to disagreements about the best form of democracy and leadership in the world.

6 It is noticeable that special interest groups frequently seek a home in the Church, and insist on being heard there, while they often cannot secure a hearing in wider society.

7 One of the causes for the failure of ministry – including Local Ministry – in some churches is the dominance of one, or a few, individuals.

8 Such institutional weakness is often linked with conceptions of Christian faith which justify it. If Christian faith means the true speaking of God which God makes possible for those who believe, this is easily

translated into the true speaking of God for the individual believer. But this overlooks the Church as the place which is so ordered as to promote true speaking of God within a community of mutual understanding and compassion, where individual voices and interests no longer need to be dominant, and where people learn from God to speak truly to each other and to the world around them.

9 'The being of God is a kind of law to his working: for that perfection which God is, giveth perfection to that he doth'; Richard Hooker, *Of the Laws of Ecclesiastical Polity*, ed. A.S. McGrade, Cambridge: Cambridge University Press, 1989, I.2.2, p. 54.

10 Faith and Order Paper No. 111, Geneva: World Council of Churches, 1982.

11 In some churches, this results in an elongated process of discernment, extended scrutiny and prior acquisition of 'experience' before people are admitted to education and ordination.

12 This is Luther's definition of sin as *incurvatus in se*.

13 These have been identified as: *results-centred*, the willingness to venture beyond familiar territory to pursue ambitious new outcomes; *internally directed*, behaving according to the deep values inherent in the task; *other-focused*, putting the collective good first; and *externally open*, learning from the environment and recognizing when change is needed. See Robert E. Quinn, 'Entering the fundamental state of leadership', *Harvard Business Review*, July–August 2005, p. 77.